My Lima Beans Are Allergic To My Spoon

My Lima Beans Are Allergic To My Spoon

My Lima Beans Are Allergic To My Spoon

Jill Schafer Boehme

To Moo and Dad,
who have loved me through many things;
and to Miss Barbara Taylor,
who nurtured the seed that God had planted.

Table of Contents

Acknowledgments

First of all, I would like to thank my daughter Rachel, who is responsible for the title of this book. In the middle of lunch one day, she really did say, "Mommy, my lima beans are allergic to my spoon." Eureka! What a great book title, thought I. And so began, over a plate of hated limas, this labor of love.

Secondly, I would be remiss not to mention Jonathan, Maggie and Spencer, who are also constant sources of inspiration.

I also have a warm "thank you" for Jamie and Sarah, my biggest cheerleaders.

And finally, I am sure I would never have completed this book at all if it weren't for my darling Eric, who pushed, encouraged, held me accountable, and took the kids out on Saturdays so that I could actually get some writing done. He is truly the love of my life.

"I can do all things through Him who strengthens me." -- Philippians 4:13

Introduction

"Hello Out There.......hello out there.......................hello out there..........................."

Surely you've felt it. That sinking, all-encompassing feeling that you are the only living adult on the planet, struggling to survive in a universe of diapers, potty chairs, goldfish snacks and Dr. Seuss. Even your husband may as well reside in a foreign country; you can recite his voice mail message by heart, and you're convinced he never checks it anyway. Even if he *does* call, his understanding of your state of mind is fairly limited.

At the very least, we, as moms, need to know that we are not alone. Across county lines and state lines; in small towns and crowded cities; in apartments and duplexes and two-story brick homes: we are all out there, striving to bring order to our lives and the very best of everything to our young brood. Despite differences in education and intellect, finances and lifestyle, and race and ethnicity, we are attached one to another with that golden cord of motherhood. We wonder if teething at three months is normal; we want someone to applaud for us when our two-year-olds finally use the toilet; we worry if our preschoolers will be stunted for life if they never eat any vegetables; and we want to know if we are the only ones who need to run into the closet and scream into an armful of slacks and dresses before we can return to our children with some sense of sanity. Threaded through all this, of course, is our intense need for affirmation: affirmation as mothers, as wives, and as women. It crosses our minds daily that we may have lost ourselves along the way, and we desperately want someone to find us and tell us that we're okay.

Allow me, fellow soldier-at-home, to help you to find yourself. Enter my world of bedwetting, lost toddlers, stretch

11

marks, and sibling rivalry. Laugh with me, cry with me, and discover that you are not alone. For every half-crazed, postpartum woman, there are hundreds more. For every unsung accomplishment of your day, there are scores of mothers just like yourself who would love to applaud for you, and for whom, I am sure, you would gladly applaud.

We have embarked on the same journey, and while our paths may swerve and diverge, our destination is the same: children who have grown into happy, well-adjusted adults. There are days on which we doubt ourselves. Indeed, there are days on which we barely make it through the dinner hour with all of our brain cells intact. And yet, somehow, we know that we wouldn't trade this life for anything.

Join me in celebrating the wonderful thing that we are doing. We are raising our children.

Pregnancy and Childbirth

Day Forty

It was an ordinary day. This is what I kept telling myself in order to keep my hopes from soaring. There had been too many ups and downs in the trying-to-get-pregnant drama of my life, and I didn't think I could bear another crash.

We were suspicious, of course. After a while you know exactly what to look for, and things looked admittedly more hopeful this time. The deal had been struck: on Day Forty, we would buy the pregnancy test.

It was dinnertime, and we were on our way home from work and errands. Just ahead, I noticed a cluster of cars and people off to the side of the road. I wondered aloud what was going on.

"President Bush is in town. Maybe his plane has just landed." Eric always knows what's going on.

We pulled over to join the small crowd that had gathered at a spot affording a decent view of the runway. Part of me wrestled with not wanting to share Day Forty with President Bush - then again, I thought it might make an interesting story some day. We could see (just barely) that Air Force One had already landed. A man beside us was standing on top of a telephone box, looking through binoculars – a serious Republican, no doubt. We asked him what he could see.

"Well, it looks like, uh....well..." He couldn't see much.

The novelty of the moment having worn off, we slipped back into the car in order to reach our true destination: the pharmacy. I tried to remain casual as I picked up the pregnancy kit and slid it onto the counter. After all, this was not the first one I had bought. I had already learned that monthly disappointment could be expensive. The middle-aged woman behind the counter smiled at me warmly.

"I hope it turns out the way you want it to!"

I thanked her, trying not to glow as I did so. I didn't think it would be appropriate to tell her that today was Day Forty. I left quietly, clutching the bag with nervous fingers.

Ten minutes later I was at home, in the bathroom. Really, I was quite a pro at this pregnancy stick thing. This time, though, I had no desire to look at the results. I couldn't stand the thought of another blank test window, and decided it would be best if Eric would read the results and break them to me gently.

"Now, this is the control window, and it's going to be pink either way. This one's the test window. If the test window is pink, it's positive. OK?" He assured me that he understood. I remained terrified that he might read it wrong.

I climbed into the bed and curled up in a fetal position. Four minutes wasn't really that long, but I needed to protect myself from the agony of waiting for what might be another disappointment. As I lay there, I told the Lord that I trusted Him, no matter what. I closed my eyes.

Four minutes passed. Eric got up and walked over to where the stick was sitting on the sink. Too many seconds went by, so I peeked. Eric was trying to pull the stick out of the plastic base.

"Just turn it around," I said with quiet intensity. Then I hid my face again.

This was too much! No one had warned me that Day Forty was going to be played out in slow motion.

Eric walked over and tapped me on the shoulder. I didn't move.

"It's pink."

"No, it's not." I still didn't move.

He tapped me again. "Yes, it is. Congratulations, Mommy!"

I sat up wordlessly and looked at Eric. He was smiling, but I wasn't ready to smile yet. The fear that he had read the test wrong would not release my heart, so I jumped up and ran over to the sink to see for myself. Everything in me wanted to believe him. Each heartbeat that occurred in the time it took me to move from the bed to the sink pulsed, "Yes! Yes!" I had to see it with my own eyes. The deep yearning, the unfulfilled longing of my heart to be a mother was too inexpressibly great to allow this moment to be anything less than what it was. I reached for the test stick and held it up to the light.

It was most decidedly pink.

The State of Being Pregnant

Life, for the average woman, has many humbling moments. I am convinced, however, that ninety percent of these moments occur when she is pregnant.

For one thing, there aren't many of us who flounce around feeling as though we have The Perfect Body. Even the most attractive women I talk to can easily find *something* they don't like about themselves. Imagine, then, taking this already-flawed perception of self and adding twenty inches and thirty-five pounds to it! Figure in the swollen ankles, huge breasts, sticking-out belly button, and ridiculous silhouette, and you can begin to see why the state of being pregnant, while nothing less than a blessing, can be a source of constant humiliation.

Think of all the things that a non-pregnant woman takes for granted – shaving her legs, for example. Now, maybe I'm neurotic, but I've always done an extra careful shaving job on obstetrician appointment days. As my first pregnancy progressed and I was able to see less and less of my legs, I soon realized that I was not going to be able to remove any hair that was growing above my knees. At first I was horrified by the thought of it – how I could possibly be expected to go to the doctor looking like that? Gradually, though, I came to terms with it. I realized that I was not the only pregnant woman who couldn't see the insides her of thighs, let alone shave them. I'm sure my doctor is used to his hairy, third-trimester clientele.

The simple act of urinating can become rather challenging as well. Bladders don't do very well when five- to seven-pound babies are smashed against them, and certain toilet acrobatics become necessary in order to void at least a few drops. I found that lifting up my belly and leaning forward with my legs spread did the trick. Of course, wiping isn't an easy feat, either. One might do better if one's arms were made of rubber. And don't even get me started on the pooping end of things...the word "hemorrhoids" still makes me wince (probably because, four babies later, I still have them).

In the midst of so many physical changes (not the least of which is an abdomen the size of a ninety-pound, prize pumpkin), you can imagine how difficult it is to feel sexy. Slipping into something teeny-weeny and sliding seductively under the covers is not quite the same as struggling into something expandable and plopping butt-first into the bed. Hard to believe that it was actually the sex act that led to this condition! How can life be so unfair? In truth, things are a bit easier when one has a sensitive husband who declares his wife's beauty regardless of her changing shape. Eric, for instance, affirmed my sexiness during all four of my pregnancies, and never complained about my changing body.

Of course, during the last trimester, he didn't come near me. I was willing to be creative (i.e., I was desperate). But for whatever reason, Eric wasn't comfortable having sex with an active baby sandwiched between us. To be fair, it isn't exactly a piece of cake to "get it together" when one partner's belly is swollen beyond recognition. A man can only arch his back so far! But the combination of hormonal swings and feeling rejected led to some tearful nights on my part.

So, a pregnant woman can't shave, can't pee, can't feel sexy. Oh, and she can't tie her shoes, either. I still remember a trip to the mall during my third pregnancy. I was waddling (yes, pregnant women really do waddle) down the corridor on my way back from the restroom. I had noticed that my sneaker was untied, but there was nothing I could do about it. Two women were approaching, and suddenly one of them piped, "Do you know that your shoe is untied?"

"Yes. I can't tie it." No use beating around the bush.

Here comes the humbling part. The woman smiled and said, "Would you like me to tie it for you?"

I know – she was being kind. But how often do adults offer to tie the shoes of other adults? Did I really want to be perceived as a pathetic pregnant woman who couldn't tie her own shoes? Or perhaps I was just a stupid pregnant woman who should have worn shoes that didn't have laces. At any rate, I thanked the woman and told her that my husband was just ahead.

Then, Eric tied my shoe for me.

Now, this may sound dichotomous, but I really loved being pregnant. Honestly! There was nothing more wondrous than the deliciously fluttery feeling of a tiny person moving about inside me. I loved hearing the baby's heartbeat at each check-up; I enjoyed shopping for maternity clothes (and receiving lots of hand-me-downs!); I remained in a state of awe and thankfulness for the miracle growing within. Pregnancy may not be a picnic, but it is definitely on my list of "life's most treasured experiences."

After a total of thirty-six months of pregnancy, I still find myself longing for it – just one more time. Somehow, the memories of hairy legs, swollen feet, and aching back don't erase the joy of what is truly the epitome of the female experience. Sometimes I swear I hear my body whispering, "Once more. Just one more time!" On other days, the chaos of my daily life drowns out the mournful sighs of my empty womb. These are the times during which my brain, which is more sensible than my uterus, declares, "Having another baby would drive you over the edge. Four children is plenty!" Eric, of course, agrees with my brain.

Still, in the deepest part of me, I dream of another baby. My body has already been stretched, pulled, bloated, and torn. Why not once more? The gift of holding that wrinkled, beautiful little person at the end of nine months is beyond description. It would definitely be worth a few months of humiliation.

Hairy legs? Untied shoelaces? A belly the size of Texas? Who cares! When all is said and done, there is nothing as wonderful as the exhilaration of being pregnant.

Except maybe the exhilaration of getting your non-pregnant body back.

What Do You Mean I Can't Have Any Chocolate?

There are two words that can strike fear into the heart of any chocolate-loving pregnant woman: gestational diabetes.

It never crossed my mind that the routine glucose test at the beginning of my third trimester would reveal a problem. The nurse's call was an unwelcome surprise: "Jill, your numbers were borderline, so we want you to go ahead and take the full glucose tolerance test."

Well, no problem! She had said "borderline." In fact, she had expounded by explaining that the numbers had recently been lowered. Had I taken the test a year earlier, I would have passed. All right, then, there was nothing to worry about. We set up an appointment for the following week.

Drinking a few ounces of the syrupy, sickeningly sweet test beverage for the routine screening is unpleasant. Swallowing an entire twelve-ounce bottle for the three-hour glucose tolerance test is enough to bring on a severe bout of queasiness. Fortunately, I was able to steel myself against my body's inclination to succumb to sugar overload while I sat through a remarkably boring morning of blood draws and urine samples at thirty-minute intervals. At the end of it all, I felt sure that I would be vindicated. Borderline, indeed!

The bad news came like a fly ball in the face: my numbers were high. I had gestational diabetes.

My initial reaction was a complete certainty that the lab had confused my results with those of the woman who had been tested on the same morning. "The first test showed that I was borderline," I protested to Eric. "How could I now suddenly have such high readings? Something has to be wrong."

Yes, something *was* wrong. My body wasn't producing enough insulin, and I had to face it. My doctor scheduled me to meet with a nutritionist in order to control my blood sugar levels through diet. By the week of the appointment, there were only six weeks left until my due date. I was consoled by the fact that even the most restrictive diet would be limited to forty-two days.

I admit I walked into the nutritionist's office with a bit of an attitude. After all, I fully expected this woman to ban me from eating chocolate and anything else remotely tasty. Nevertheless, within the first five minutes I realized that I was dealing with someone from another planet.

While mapping out my daily diet plan, she mentioned that I would have to drink eight ounces of milk at lunchtime. I immediately informed her that I hated milk. In fact, there was no way that I could possibly drink it, so we would have to come up with an alternative calcium choice.

Ms. Nutritionist looked at me uncomprehendingly, as though she had never before met anyone who didn't like milk. Blandly, she informed me that I could drink skim milk instead: "Lots of pregnant women who can't tolerate milk seem to do fine with skim."

Clearly she had misunderstood me. "No," I insisted. "I can't drink skim milk. I can't drink *any* milk. It makes me sick!" I would have gone on to say that I had hated milk ever since I was a small girl, but I didn't think that would have made an impact. Ms. Nutritionist was dumbfounded by my inability to accept milk into my diet. I was sure that she didn't know what to do next.

In her already-flustered state, Ms. Nutritionist suddenly stopped in mid-sentence, gazing in horror at a spot in the room somewhere above my head.

"It's a bug," she announced, jumping up from her chair and batting wildly at the air. Eric and I exchanged glances as a harmless fly swooped through the air between us.

Ms. Nutritionist's half-mad eyes rested definitively on my husband. "You kill it," she commanded. "That's what men are for – they're bug slayers!" I mustered a phony laugh, and wondered if we needed to slip quietly from the room while Ms. Nutritionist wrestled with her own demons.

"Bug slayers!" she repeated, obviously hoping that Eric would rally to her cause. When the hapless insect finally vanished from sight, Ms. Nutritionist was able to settle back into her seat and resume the task at hand. Eric the Bug Slayer was quickly forgotten.

If I had had an ounce of respect for her up to this point, my confidence in her was now completely eroded.

Every question I asked seemed to throw her off. I asked her why peanut butter was allowed when it was loaded with refined sugar (she didn't know). I pointed out that ketchup also had sugar added (she seemed amazed). I begged for permission to have a few vanilla wafers once in a while, to which I received a resounding "no." Vanilla wafers were listed right in the booklet she had handed me, but she couldn't seem to read it properly.

I couldn't wait to get out of that office. It felt as though someone had just played a huge joke on me.

Thus began my six weeks of a highly restrictive diet. No more than four ounces of meat for dinner (that's a piece of meat about the size of a deck of playing cards). Crackers with one ounce of low-fat cheese for a mid-morning snack. No Coke. No chocolate. No butter on my vegetables. No flavor in my mouth.

Two good things came of these weeks of food hell. First of all, I learned to drink my coffee without sugar, and have done so ever since. Secondly, I was able to avoid the final trimester weight gain that many pregnant women fall prey to. Yes, I felt deprived. There is no substitute for chocolate. This was a small price to pay, though, to ensure the health of my baby.

Five days before my scheduled induction, some friends came over for dinner, and presented us with a turtle pie for dessert. My mouth watered as I beheld praline ice cream with caramel and chocolate in a graham cracker piecrust – with whipped cream on top. I don't think there is any woman, pregnant or non-pregnant, who could have said "no" to such a slice of decadence.

So, I didn't say "no." And about an hour later I felt as though someone had injected raw sugar into my bloodstream. It is truly amazing how our bodies adjust to whatever diet we subject them to. My entire nervous system began doing cartwheels. The thought of another slice of that dreadful pie was worse than the thought of drinking a glass of skim milk.

An unexplained phenomenon of gestational diabetes is the fact that it tends to occur in every other pregnancy. So, while my second and fourth pregnancies were completely healthy, my third one once again shot up my blood sugar levels. This time, I had to prick my finger after each meal in order to take a sugar reading. After only a few days of this distasteful routine, there wasn't a fingertip remaining that wasn't tender. I began to flinch as I anticipated each new prick.

Reluctantly, I pulled out my old diet chart and began to grumble my way through each meal. I resented having to explain to the nurse that a particularly high reading after breakfast one morning was due to the fact that I had eaten Frosted Flakes. Honestly, who can eat shredded wheat every morning without a single break? At least I hadn't eaten any chocolate.

Fortunately, the baby came two weeks early. I think my body was simply revolting: "Enough! Get this kid out of here!"

I would love to claim that my experience has left me with better eating habits. Like many mothers, though, I often feed my children more healthy food than I myself eat. I don't think I could survive without my daily Coke ration, and the inclusion of chocolate in my life goes without saying. I am truly thankful for my health and the health of my children. Having been faced with less-than-perfect pregnancies serves to remind me how truly blessed I am to have four healthy children.

I would have walked through fire to protect the health of my unborn children. Saying "no" to chocolate for a few weeks was a small sacrifice, indeed.

No More Private Parts

Did you come through the ordeal of childbirth feeling as though the term "private parts" no longer applied to you? You are not alone.

New mothers-to-be are fully aware of what parts of their bodies will be involved in the arduous task of giving birth. There are diagrams to read, classes to take, and even graphic videos to watch. "Vagina," "cervix," and "perineum" become every-day words, having long lost their power to produce a blush. Yet, truly, the reality of what our bodies are about to experience never hits home with any of us...until after the fact.

I was fortunate enough to have an acquaintance who worked as a labor and delivery nurse in the hospital in which I was to birth my first child. She was "on call" along with my doctor, and knowing that she would be there gave me an added sense of security. When I went into labor the night before I was scheduled for an induction, she prepared one of the "nicer" LDR suites for me, and waited for my arrival. I still remember seeing her smiling face as I was wheeled into the room.

The first hint that the rules of etiquette had changed came shortly after my arrival, as we were discussing my bathroom habits. Without blinking, I proudly informed her that, moments earlier, I had relieved my bowels in the toilet. It never crossed my mind that this wasn't the kind of thing I would normally share with her over dinner. Knowing how important it was to have empty intestines, all I could think of at the time was that I had done a good job; not only had I cleared the way for an accident-free delivery, I had done so in the middle of a contraction.

Labor progressed, the epidural was administered, and my "private nurse" continued to care for me, each time informing me in her gentle, Southern drawl, "I'm going to touch your bottom now." (It wasn't until I moved to the South that I heard the term "bottom" applied to the "front" of my private parts. "Bottom" always meant "rear-end;" but I suppose that's another story.) Finally, it was time to start pushing. I hunkered down, breathed deeply, and pushed with all my might. At the end of that first round, and without missing a beat, my friend whisked away the sterile pad on which I lying, and replaced it with a fresh one.

Despite my previously emptied intestines, I had most definitely "delivered" something other than my baby.

Moments like this are quickly lost on a laboring woman, and for the next hour I thought of nothing but pushing my baby into the world. After he arrived, healthy and beautiful, I lay chatting lightly with those in attendance while the doctor deftly stitched the slight tear in my perineum. It isn't often that I lie spread-eagled and exposed to the world while engaging in small talk. What made the situation most peculiar is that, at the time, it never crossed my mind that I was the only person in the room who was undressed from the waist down. The childbirth manuals don't get into these intimate details.

After having sent the baby off to the nursery in Daddy's arms, I turned to the next order of business, which was emptying my bladder. After a successful catheterization, the nurses were willing to allow me to move to a private room, with the understanding that I would have to urinate on my own fairly soon. I was still so numb from the epidural, I didn't think I'd ever be able to do it. Desperately wanting to get to my room, I kept this thought to myself.

I slept a little, nursed my baby a little, and soon the sun had risen. In came the morning shift nurse, who was seriously concerned about whether I had urinated. I had not. She sent for another nurse, who arrived bearing – I kid you not – an adult-sized potty chair on wheels. I was helped onto the offensive throne, and there I sat, on the potty, while two nurses and my husband watched with baited breath.

Have you ever tried to pee on command? I could not produce a drop. Even in my I'm-exhausted-I've-just-given-birth state of mind, I was fully aware of how embarrassing a situation this was. Suddenly I was able to relate to every potty-training toddler on the planet. I wondered if I would get some M-and-M's if I performed the task.

"Sometimes running the tap helps," chirped one of the helpful nurses, as she reached for the faucet. Was she serious? My performance was certainly not going to be improved by adding sound effects. Relieving myself in front of an audience was simply out of the question.

Finally, they left me alone, and much to everyone's relief, I was able to empty my bladder in the privacy of the bathroom. At the very least, someone should have sent me flowers to congratulate me…but all the flowers were for the new baby.

On the second morning, the pediatrician arrived just as I was preparing to get into the shower. There I stood, hair disheveled, wearing a wrinkled hospital gown, and he was giving me a hug. I would never have answered the door at home in that condition, let alone allow someone to hug me. Yet, considering all I had been through, it didn't seem to matter. Later, I had to put down my hair dryer when my obstetrician arrived, so that he could "check my bottom." I suppose I could have asked him to just have a peek while I finished drying my hair. Maybe he would have enjoyed watching me urinate in the potty-on-wheels.

Bringing home my new baby was coupled with leaving behind my old self; the self that kept her bathroom habits private; the self that remained fully dressed around strangers; the self that didn't engage in many conversations about female organs. Nothing was sacred. I was a fully exposed woman; and now that I was nursing, I was to become even more so. Exposing my breasts to a lactation consultant so that she could teach me how to get rid of my baby's "click" was on par with what had happened in the hospital, albeit less graphic.

And now you know the source of my irreverence. Every woman who has given birth has gone through this rite of passage. Whether the birth occurs at home, in a hospital, or on the freeway, a laboring woman's body takes over, and there is no room for modesty. We all have the same body parts; they all do the same things; and, once we've been through childbirth, innumerable people have observed us in ways we've never dreamed.

How do we recover? For the first six weeks, we rest, heal, and don't think about it. Then, we begin to realize that we are no less precious or beautiful for having been necessarily humbled during childbirth. Most importantly, when we have sensitive husbands who affirm our womanhood after we fear that all has been lost, we have a sporting chance at feeling female again….and perhaps even slightly sexy!

Rest easy, new mommies. You will feel whole and beautiful again. Your bodies have done an amazing task – one that they have been divinely designed to do. Give yourself credit for having gone through it, and enjoy the freedom of perhaps having a few less hang-ups about your body than you may have had before.

30

And if you ever invite me for dinner, please don't ask me to pee for your guests.

Labor? No Sweat

Sometimes we are absolutely convinced that we are pros. Whatever the task, talent, or skill, we have told ourselves that, yes, indeed, we've got this one all wrapped up: another slice of the proverbial "piece of cake." And so it was when I went into labor with my fourth child. I had been there, done that. Three onsets of labor, three sessions of timing contractions, three trips to the hospital, three epidurals, and three vaginal births were all on my maternity resume. I was undaunted by Number Four.

As was my usual wont, I stayed away from the hospital as long as I comfortably could. Granted, babies do tend to come more quickly with each subsequent birth, but I felt confident in my ability to assess labor. Eric and I arrived at the hospital at around ten o'clock at night. Discovering that I was only four to five centimeters dilated was a letdown; during Labor Three I had arrived at the hospital at eight centimeters, and the entire nursing staff had been amazed that I wasn't yelling in pain. (Of course, my first question had been, "Can I still get an epidural?" I could not imagine birth as anything but a painless, smiling procedure.)

I settled into my routine of "hee-hee" breathing and posing for pictures. It was easy to comfort myself with the knowledge that soon the anesthesiologist would be arriving with her blessed needle and tubes, and thirty minutes later I would be blissfully numb. She arrived, and I curled up into the required fetal position. The few minutes of discomfort are well worth the results, so, as I had done three times before, I willed myself to relax and breathe.

She was doing an awful lot of poking, and I began to wonder if perhaps this was her first epidural. Patience is one thing I completely lack while in the midst of any amount of pain. After what seemed to me like a rather clumsy entry, the needle was in place, and I felt the warm rush of medicine.

Countdown to sheer pleasure. I knew that I would feel five or six more contractions, and nothing more.

Thirty minutes later, I was still in pain. This was unexpected, but not without remedy. I received a second dose of medicine. Having had a similar experience during Labor One, I was not overly concerned.

The pain continued. Heee-heee-hoooooo. Heee-heee-hoooooo. I flipped into denial. This wasn't really happening. I didn't HAVE babies this way. My deliveries were always painless!

I couldn't wish it away. My husband and I both had to swallow the truth: I was going to deliver without medication.

"Ice chips," I croaked to my husband. He lovingly placed one on my tongue.

I wasn't having fun. This wasn't supposed to happen! I didn't really care if women gave birth this way for countless centuries; the fact remained that I did not give birth this way. I wasn't prepared.

It was time to push. Somewhere in the midst of my experience I had come up with the idea that once pushing began, there wasn't any more pain. I couldn't have been more deluded.

Somebody was helping me prop my legs up. Surely they didn't expect me to push against this horrendous pain! This was inhumane. I could breathe through it, but there was no way I could *push* through it.

"OK, push!"

They had to be joking.

"I CAN'T!" I screamed. What a ridiculous thing to scream. Did I think they were going to let me off the hook at that point?

"Yes, yes, you can do it!" Oh, nice. Cheerleaders in the delivery room. Where was my husband?

I pushed. I yelled. I yelled more than I pushed. I don't think I ever screamed so loudly in my life.

The anesthesiologist was cringing in a far corner. Her evening was not off to a good start.

Round two began.

My eyes were closed. I yelled with every cubic inch of oxygen in my lungs. Somehow during that completely incoherent process, I gave birth.

The nurse placed my son on my belly. I couldn't focus on him; my eyes kept crossing. I was trembling all over.

"Loooooooook, look at your little boy!" My what? What did she want me to look at?

Eric soon came into view, all smiles. The escapade was over; our second son had arrived, healthy and beautiful.

I was beginning to gather my wits about me. Little Spencer Michael wiggled and twitched in my arms, the way newborns do. We were both going to be all right. I had survived the unanticipated, and I held my prize in my arms. My consolation was that the passage of time would soon erase the memory of my unexpected natural childbirth. I was feeling better already. One day soon, this would be in the distant past.

Eric sat down in a chair beside the bed, video camera in hand. I was contented by the thought of his having put down the camera in order to support me through my time of duress. Then, like a rock through a pane of glass, his words shattered my fantasy.

"I got it all on tape!"

I was too weak to strangle him. All I could do was stare at him in disbelief.

"You didn't! I was yelling...I was screaming! I don't ever want anyone to see that! I don't ever want to see that myself! Please tell me you didn't film all that!"

He had.

More than two years passed before I was able to watch the video. The not-so-instant replay of my ordeal didn't do much for my self-image. (Let's just say that it was less than glamorous.) Even though my husband still praises me for being "a trooper," I think that, ultimately, I would rather not be reminded.

I no longer claim to be a pro.

Sex After Childbirth

I was standing in a friend's kitchen trying to engage in idle conversation with women I didn't know. My husband and I had been invited for an evening of games and refreshments, and back then I would rather have crawled under the sofa than play a game with a room full of strangers. At any rate, there I stood, listening to the chatter around me and trying to chime in.

One woman in the crowd was particularly interested in my friend's sex life. She and her husband were newly married, and the thought of what pregnancy would do to her body was causing her husband to loathe the idea of ever becoming a father.

"I mean, is it the same afterward?" this young wife asked in earnest. "Because, well, my husband is afraid that...well, that it will stretch me all out down there, and...and that it won't be the same afterward."

My friend, whose baby was five months old, had nothing to offer. "I had a C-section," she piped. "So I can't answer your question."

There I stood, four months into my first pregnancy. I had no words of wisdom to offer this worried woman. Of course, I couldn't help thinking that her husband had to be one of the most insensitive men on earth. During my quest to become pregnant, Eric had never once made me feel like becoming a mother would ruin my sex life. I was sure that this couple's fears were unfounded, yet my own experience had not yet encompassed the realm of post-birth sex. Out of necessity, I remained silent.

If only I had known then what I now know. After all these years, I still long to return to that moment in time in order to allay that couple's misguided fears: "Yes, your body will change. But it will heal and regain strength after childbirth, and sex can be as fantastic as ever!"

Sex wasn't at the top of my list after Jonathan was born. I was sore and tired, and, as far as I was concerned, my suddenly mammoth breasts were reserved for my newborn. Still, I longed for a day on which I would feel more like my old self. Although the official "postpartum" healing period is six weeks, my doctor told me that sex would be fine as soon as the bleeding and discomfort had stopped. And so we waited.

On the Big Night, I asked my husband, "Please....treat me like a virgin."

Imagine the position in which I had just put my husband! The woman with whom he'd been having sex for almost four years was asking him to put all that aside and act like they'd never done it before. Still, I knew that my body was tender, and I had been warned that sex might be uncomfortable for a while. I was counting on Eric to treat me gently; to coax me back to where I had been before the pregnancy.

Yes, he was gentle. And yes, it hurt, anyway. Soon, though, the discomfort faded, and before long our sex life was very much as it had always been. My body had not been "ruined" by childbirth.

There was an added distraction, though, for which I hadn't been prepared: my breasts leaked. Now, any breastfeeding mom can attest to the fact that, in the early months, breasts are prone to leaking. This wasn't a little drop here and there, though – this was a stream of breastmilk pouring from each breast, running down the sides of my body and soaking the sheets beneath me.

How is a woman supposed to feel sexy with breastmilk dribbling all over the bed?

I was much more bothered by this phenomenon than my husband was. I really think he found it quite amusing. I wasn't so sure, though, that I wanted to be found amusing while I was in bed with my husband. I preferred to be found desirable. Let's face it: who wants to be laughed at in the middle of sex?

The leaking breast syndrome recurred with each subsequent baby. Like every other aspect of pregnancy and childbirth, it was a phase that came and went without fanfare. My breasts may now be one-fourth their lactating size, but at least they remain dry during intercourse.

What it comes down to is this: if a husband and wife can maintain a sense of humor during the changes that take place following the birth of a child, their relationship will have a much better chance of remaining unscathed. Laughter and patience have carried Eric and me through many a trial. Neither one of us denies that my body is vastly different from the way it was when we first married. Yes, a vagina can feel a little more "roomy" after it produces a few eight-pound babies. Yes, the slightest whimper from a baby in the next room can cause a passion-filled mommy to become suddenly cold. And yes, young children *will* walk through unlocked bedroom doors in the midst of foreplay. The ability to take everything in stride ensures the continuance of a loving relationship between spouses.

It falls to the woman, though, to ultimately take responsibility for the health and strength of her own body. I admit that my husband is a bigger fan of Kegel* exercises than I am. I find them tedious and annoying, despite the fact that they do make a difference. Using Kegel exercises to strengthen the muscle tone of the vagina is one way to improve post-birth sex. General physical exercise is beneficial as well, although the thought of exercising on purpose makes me break out in hives.

The biggest boost to my sexuality comes from my husband. Throughout four pregnancies and postpartum periods, and all the times in between, Eric has unconditionally loved me and made me feel beautiful. Imagine that: a thirty-something mother of four whose stomach is stretched beyond recognition has a husband who finds her beautiful!

A woman who feels beautiful *is* beautiful.

Childbirth does not kill sex lives. If it did, I would today be the mother of only one child. My relationship with Eric is complex and ever-changing; if we did not make it a priority, our marriage would not survive. Having a husband who adores me (and some days that must be a stretch for him) is one of the solid foundations of happiness in my life. I am not only a mother – I am the wife, friend, and lover of my beloved spouse. Through the physical celebration of my love for him, I am energized and affirmed as a woman. I may not be a flat-bellied, big-breasted bombshell – but to Eric, I am gorgeous.

If I could learn to love every flabby, squooshy, stretched-out bit of my body as much as my husband does, I would be a confident, emotionally healthy woman, indeed!

Accept the changes in your body. Do what you can to strengthen the weak parts. And allow your husband to embrace you without trepidation. You are still the woman he married. Your body may have changed, but your sexy, vibrant, passionate self is very much the same. Don't be afraid to let her out.

* To perform Kegel exercises, firmly tense the muscles around your vagina and anus. Hold for ten seconds, then slowly release. Repeat. Do at least twenty-five repetitions a day, while sitting, standing, or lying on your back.

When Do I Get My Body Back?

All right, you say. I've survived the embarrassment of childbirth. I have rested, taken my vitamins, and enjoyed thousands of precious moments with my newborn. So, when do I get my body back?

During my first pregnancy, my husband splurged and bought me an over-priced Laura Ashley jumper. I had been enthralled with it in the store, mostly because the pregnant sales clerk was wearing an identical one. Who would have dreamed that a pregnant woman could wear something by Laura Ashley? Indeed, the high waistline, which I normally despised, lent itself perfectly to the swollen state of pregnancy. I found the jumper under my pillow that night (Eric had quietly purchased it while I was browsing in another store), and I wore it until the buttons were straining and the weather grew too warm.

When my son was five months old, I pulled the jumper out of my closet, thrilled to be able to wear it in my non-pregnant state. The button-down front worked well for breastfeeding, and the high waistline helped to camouflage (so I thought) my still squishy and bulging tummy. I felt cute and comfortable as we left for church that morning.

After having picked Jonathan up from the nursery, we were riding the elevator up to the main floor of our church building with a woman whom we did not know. She smiled warmly at our son and asked, "How old is he?"

"Five months," I smiled back.

Then came the bombshell. The woman gestured toward my stomach and said, "And when's THIS one due?"

I felt my whole body go numb, and I wasn't quite able to make eye contact with her. "It's not," I replied. The opening elevator door provided immediate escape.

I'm sure the woman was as embarrassed as I was – probably more so. Even in my moment of utter horror, I honestly did not want to make her uncomfortable. Still, I was indignant. Do the math, I thought to myself. My son is five months old – how could I POSSIBLY be pregnant enough to be showing already if my son is only five months old??

The Laura Ashley jumper was hastily returned to my closet.

While it is true, indeed, that breastfeeding helps to melt off the post-pregnancy pounds (as long as you're not eating a box of chocolate every day), the weight loss does not guarantee a return of the pre-pregnancy shape. Somehow, everything shifts. For those of us who are not inclined to submit our bodies to the daily torture of high-impact work-outs, that means a slightly thicker waistline, some extra skin here and there, and definitely a change in silhouette.

The infamous jumper returned to favor during my second pregnancy, when I was once again able to wear it until the season change. After that, it was relegated to my archive of maternity clothes. I was not going to make the same mistake twice.

Three weeks after the birth of my daughter, we spent the day at the local zoo. While we were there, we met up with a family with whom we were acquainted at church. Aware that I had been expecting a baby, the woman said, with great empathy, "Don't worry. It'll be here before you know it." Once again, I froze. This was worse than the elevator encounter: this was someone that I knew! Didn't she notice the blatant fact that, despite my physical condition, I was pushing a baby stroller?

After a brief hesitation, I gestured a bit frenetically toward the stroller where Maggie lay sleeping. "Here she is!" I announced. I admit, at that point I felt much more badly for my friend than I did for myself. It was she, after all, who had committed the faux pas. The only thing I was guilty of was an enlarged abdomen.

Of course, the one thing that tended to offset the thickness-in-the-middle of those early months was the gargantuan pair of breasts bestowed upon me as a breastfeeding woman. Wearing cup sizes of which I had not previously known the existence, I felt somehow that this was a reward meant to be savored for a time. Being able to look down and see a real cleavage was a new experience for me. And, of course, the large bustline helped to hide a waistline that stubbornly refused to humble itself.

I had always assumed that my breasts, once they were no longer employed by my baby, would settle back into their own size and shape. After the weaning of my firstborn, they eventually did. There is a biological fact, however, of which I was blissfully unaware at the time: there is no muscle in our breasts. Once they are "stretched out" from a pregnancy or two, there is no way to "tone them up" again. After having delivered and nursed four children, I can honestly say that, should National Geographic need a stand-in for one of those topless natives in Zimbabwe, I'm their woman.

For a while, I was in some level of denial about this new state of my breasts. It wasn't until I adventurously tried on a push-up bra after the weaning of my third baby that the truth hit. "This will perk me up," I told myself. Then, I looked down in horror: the bra cups were half empty. My breasts filled the bottom half like so much eggnog in a glass. Reality set in: I didn't have anything left to "push up!"

Now, before you slunk off to a corner in despair, please understand that I have not come to the conclusion – and nor should you – that pregnancy means certain death to the beauty of your body. Not at all! It simply becomes necessary to accept the fact that your body will be different. That is not an excuse, of course, to become a physical wreck and blame it on the baby: "Oh, you know, I used to be a size 8, but now I'm a size 18. That's what motherhood does to you." There are a variety of factors that might "do that" to you, but "motherhood" should not be listed among them.

Eating wisely and staying moderately active will go a long way in bringing your figure back into acceptable parameters. One thing we all have to learn to accept is that having a hard, flat tummy is something that society has created and dubbed "sexy." If we take a look at Baroque art, we see a completely different model of what was once considered desirable: well-rounded ladies with small, dangling breasts, and stomachs that look as though they've spent their lives giving birth. "Yuck!" you say. Evidently, Baroque gentlemen would disagree, as would, I believe, the ladies themselves. A close look at these Baroque beauties reveals content - even sultry - smiles, as though they are aware of their own charms. Would that we women of the twenty-first century would learn to feel as confident about our bodies!

When will you get your body back? Ask instead, "When will I feel good about my body?" Once you lose the weight (and yes, I think it's very important that you do) and determine what level of physical fitness you are comfortable with, you must then take stock of what you have. Are you healthy? Does most of your old clothing fit you? Do you have energy? And does your husband still think you're the most beautiful woman on the face of the earth? If so, then accept yourself as you are, and embrace your body's mild marks of motherhood with thankfulness, and perhaps a degree of pride. Think of the marvelous feat your body has accomplished – carrying, delivering, and nurturing another human being. What more wondrous thing could there possibly be? Your body has brought forth and sustained new life. Do not chastise it for having a few battle scars.

At worst, being a Baroque Beauty can't be all that bad.

Losing Jeremy

I was absolutely certain that I was pregnant.

Unlike the first time, when my husband had been very involved in my cycle and the possibility that conception had occurred, I kept quiet. Jonathan was thirteen months old; I had already calculated that the new baby would be born in February, three months before Jonathan's second birthday. I knew that my body was whispering, "I'm pregnant!" at every turn, yet I had to verify it before making the big announcement.

It was a Saturday afternoon. Jonathan was asleep; Eric was busy at the computer. I slipped into the bathroom and took the pregnancy test. One – two – three – four minutes passed. I held my breath and looked at the test stick. It was positive. My body hadn't lied to me.

Oh, the elation of knowing that another new life was growing inside me! I wanted to bask in the moment for a while – alone. I glided out the back door into the sunshine of what was suddenly a glorious afternoon. "I'm pregnant.....I'm pregnant...." I whispered to myself. I can still feel the gravel beneath the soles of my pink slippers as I sauntered around and around the driveway. "I'm pregnant!"

Boundless joy is not easily contained, so I soon presented myself in the bedroom where Eric sat working.

"I have something to tell you."

Eric was shocked. Caught unprepared. Then, moments later, he was smiling. "We" were pregnant!

I knew the pregnancy was very new; so new, in fact that my doctor's office didn't even want to see me for another month. Undaunted, I made the appointment. I was eager to once again delve into the world of maternity clothes, fetal acrobatics, and prenatal vitamins. Oh, the delight of being pregnant once again!

Somehow, I was convinced from the start that I was carrying another boy – a brother for Jonathan. And so I named him Jeremy. Jonathan and Jeremy. Jeremy and Jonathan. I was completely, irrevocably attached to the tiny baby inside of me.

Daily I was bursting with the well-kept secret of this pregnancy. One night, just five days after the Big Announcement, Eric and I lay cuddling in bed, chatting about how just that day at work he had circumvented a "so, when is Jill going to have another baby" question. I giggled in his arms, radiant with the knowledge of what lay hidden within me. Soon we would announce it to the world.

Again it was Saturday. My new baby had grown seven days bigger inside me. Jonathan was strapped into his car seat, ready to accompany us to Eric's company picnic. The car was already running; I simply had to run inside to make a quick trip to the bathroom before we left.

There was blood in my panties.

I froze, staring at the small oval of blood on my pantiliner. I immediately knew that something was wrong. It didn't matter that the books claimed that spotting can be normal for many women during pregnancy. I had never spotted during my first pregnancy. This wasn't "normal" for me.

I knew with a rush of sick dread and certainty that I was losing this baby.

Numb, I ran out to the car where Eric sat waiting.

"Eric, I'm bleeding."

At first, Eric wasn't as concerned as I was. An incurable optimist, he tried to reassure me that it was probably nothing. I was not convinced. I knew that I shouldn't be bleeding.

A call to my doctor's office was less than reassuring. "Well, put your feet up and rest for the remainder of the day, to see if the bleeding stops. It could very well be normal. If you are losing the baby, though, there isn't anything we can do to stop that."

I desperately tried to will my body to stop bleeding. The bleeding continued; it grew heavier. Oh, Jeremy, Jeremy....don't leave me. don't die.....

By Sunday it was clear that I was losing the baby. The blood was so heavy that at times it would run down my legs when I got up off of the toilet. Curled up on the floor in my bedroom, I sobbed, my arms cradling my afflicted abdomen. Jeremy........Jeremy.......

On Monday Eric drove me to the obstetrician's office, where I received all the necessary blood tests. Afterward, the doctor who had delivered Jonathan spoke gentle words of encouragement to me: "There wasn't anything that you did to cause this. Miscarriage is a normal part of the reproductive cycle."

Eric the Optimist wasn't willing to let go of his wife's dream. "But," he said to the doctor, "Jill's temperature is still up. So, couldn't it...?" He trailed off. The doctor explained to Eric what I already knew: the pregnancy hormones were still present in my body, and wouldn't drop off for a couple more days. Hence, the elevated basal body temperature.

Two days later I had to return for another quick blood draw, which would confirm the return of my hormones to normal. Somehow I got lost in the queue and sat, forlorn and forgotten, in the waiting room, surrounded by pregnant women. Taking note of a sign that read, "If you have been waiting for more than thirty minutes, please let us know," I returned to the window.

"Excuse me, I'm just here to have blood drawn, and I've been waiting for half an hour."

Instead of trying to help me, the woman gave me a lame excuse. I returned to my seat, too crushed and despondent to fight. The minutes ticked by; the pregnant women paraded by. It was the worst waiting room experience of my life. Finally, a very apologetic nurse called me in.

"I am SO SORRY, Jill. You should have been taken care of right away."

I tried to smile my appreciation. Smiling, to me, was a forgotten art. The blood draw took two minutes, and I was free to leave. There was nothing left to do.

Except one thing.

I had to grieve. Oh, how I grieved. I grieved the loss of this baby as I had never grieved anything before. The deaths that had occurred in my life had been, to this point, relatively meaningless – grandparents and other relatives with whom I had had little or no relationship. This was different. I felt the loss of this baby deep within my spirit, as if a living piece of my soul had been ripped from me, and was bleeding endlessly. Jeremy, whose heart had not even begun to beat when he left me, had been as much my child as if I had carried him to term and delivered him, healthy and whole.

Oh, Jeremy......why?

It is so easy now to look back and say, "Well, my goodness, if Jeremy had been born, I wouldn't have my Maggie!" For, indeed, within three months of having lost Jeremy, I was pregnant again, and this time I gave birth to a healthy baby – not a brother for Jonathan, but a sweet, dimple-cheeked sister. Yet, at the time, there was no minimizing the pain of having lost that little baby – the child whom I would never hold in my arms.

The fact that many women have miscarriages does not serve to comfort us when we walk through one ourselves. It is true that, were it not for the advent of modern pregnancy tests, I would most likely never have known I was pregnant in the first place. No matter: I did know. I rejoiced, I loved, I lost, I grieved. For whatever reason, it was something I needed to walk through.

Have you lost a baby? I am deeply sorry. Have you grieved your loss? It is no small thing – whether you were six weeks pregnant or six months pregnant, you have lost a precious, irreplaceable thing. Weep for your lost child; then release him, so that you can move on.

Sweet, tiny Jeremy – for seven days, I loved you. You were no less a child for the brevity of your existence. And I am no less a woman for struggling with the loss. I release you, little one.

Baby Tales

Ugly Babies

Newborn babies are not pretty.

To the blinded eye of a new grandparent; to the stunned vision of a brand-new father; to the weary, loving gaze of a woman who has just given birth - a newborn may indeed appear perfect. I am here to assure you, however, that a new baby is not going to win any awards for beauty.

My first glimpse of Jonathan's face came when his head crowned during birth. The nurse wheeled a freestanding mirror into place, and I gazed enraptured at my new little son's face. Cradled between my legs and covered in the slime of childbirth, it was nothing less than magnificent to behold.

"Look at his little face!" I breathed.

Several minutes later, when I first held him in my arms, I was able, with tentative eyes and fingers, to examine him more closely.

His nose was dented.

Yes, even in the glow of becoming a new mommy, I saw that pushed-in nose. Whether there was a mysterious kink in my birth canal or whether the soft, new nose couldn't handle the final moments of pushing, the effects of Jonathan's entry into the world were glaringly noticeable.

But that wasn't all. There was a distinct, red mark on his right eyelid. His hands were blue. And that pushed-in nose was covered in tiny, white bumps. Naturally, I couldn't have loved him more. Here in my arms was the essence of my dreams - my deepest desire fulfilled. If beauty is in the eye of the beholder, then, yes, indeed he was beautiful. Not known for being delusional, however, I was quite able to point out his many flaws - without neglecting to fall more madly in love with him as each minute passed.

Time eases many things, including the marks of childbirth on a new baby. By three months, Jonathan qualified for Baby-of-the-Year. His nose was perfect, his skin was smooth, his smile could melt a glacier. Hard critic that I am, it was easy to admit that I definitely had a beautiful baby.

If you haven't already noticed, I am not of the "all babies are beautiful" school. Years before any of mine were born, I once met up with an ex-coworker who had recently given birth to her first baby. Her eagerness to show off her firstborn was apparent by the way she grabbed my shirt and pulled me toward the baby stroller. I was all smiles as I peered beneath the stroller's canopy.

Inside was the ugliest baby I had ever seen.

I almost choked as I tried to come up with a gracious response to the strange-faced child with the disproportionate mop of hair on his head.

"My, he has a lot of hair!"

Regardless of whether I am beholding someone's prize-and-joy, be-all-end-all firstborn, I will not call something beautiful that is not.

I am a product, I suppose, of a culture that values beauty over more intrinsic values. Neither my husband nor I belong to the class of "beautiful people," and before my children were born I spent a lot of time agonizing over how they would look. I was terrified that I would end up with children cursed with the worst features from both sides of our families (and you should see some of the specimens related to my husband!). Despite the fact that I have always known that character carries greater weight than looks, I still find myself obsessing about my children's' appearances.

Silly, isn't it?

I delight in the accomplishments of my son, yet I wonder if the cat-scratch scar under his right eye will be visible when he is an adult. I bask in the warmth of my toddler's grin, yet I worry that he will grow up to look too much like his daddy and not enough like my father (who was quite handsome in his youth). I am tickled as I watch my daughters playing dress-up, yet I secretly fear that one will be more beautiful than the other when they are grown.

Am I the only one who has thoughts like this?

Let's face it - this isn't a topic we are likely to bring up around the coffee table. We are all quick to discuss our children's' developmental milestones, latest interests, and the day-to-day struggles of sibling rivalry and messy bedrooms. Ask us to share our deepest thoughts, though, and most of us will hide inside ourselves. "I must be the only mother in this room who thinks her daughter's crooked nose will ruin her chances of a happy marriage, so I'd better keep quiet." "Sally's daughter is really odd-looking, and Emma's boys look like fat little trolls. I wonder what the other moms think of my two kids?" "My boy is the most handsome one in here, but he keeps picking his nose and wiping the boogies on his shirt. I am mortified!"

Then, of course, there are the piles of newborn photos that we must succumb to when our best friend or neighbor or sister plops them in our lap. It's hard enough to smile your way through twenty-four or a hundred or five thousand poorly done snapshots of someone else's kid, but trying to come up with positive comments when you can't see a single attractive feature is a daunting task, indeed! My favorites are the out-of-focus, red-eye shots that convince the viewer that the child in the picture is definitely possessed by demons. There are also the hospital shots that display pose after pose of a pinkish or brownish blob in a pile of blanket, held by a grinning New Dad or New Mom or New Grandmother or New Brother or any other "new" person that may have been present during the hospital stay. After the first two or three photos, the phrase "Ohh, how cute!" starts to wear a bit thin. Especially if the baby isn't that cute.

What am I really saying here? I am saying that, ultimately, it doesn't matter. You are allowed to think that your newborn is the most beautiful thing on the planet (as long as you wake up and smell the coffee at some point). You are also allowed to think that your sister-in-law's baby is ugly (as long as you don't tell her that). The children we raise need to be people of character, not empty shells. The doubts and worries I have had over the years concerning my children's appearance are thoughts that I have never conveyed to them. A child - any child - is more than the sum total of his "beautiful parts." The gifts and traits that our Loving Creator has instilled in our children, coupled with the values and good habits in which we train them, matter far more than what color their eyes are or how tall they've grown.

So, when that new baby arrives in your arms all bent and squished and dented and marked, don't despair! You are beholding an imperfect yet remarkable creature who, under your loving guidance, will grow to make his mark on this world. And if someone should say, "So, how old is he?" instead of "Oh, he's gorgeous," just smile and answer the question. For deep in your heart you know that your baby is a one-in-a-billion prize, and the beauty within him will grow in proportion to the love and care he receives.

"Your adornment must not be merely external – braiding the hair, and wearing gold jewelry, or putting on dresses; but let it be the hidden person of the heart, with the imperishable quality of a gentle and quiet spirit, which is precious in the sight of God." (1 Peter 3:3-4)

If "beautiful" can be defined as "the potential planted inside each new being," then yes, indeed, all new babies are "beautiful."

Udders Must Be Easier

Breastfeeding is a learned art. Neither mother nor child comes to the experience with an innate sense of exactly how to do it. Although I have always believed this – indeed, I have experienced this – to be true, there is one vital fact that I had, until the birth of my fourth child, overlooked: even though Mommy may have prior experience, this does not guarantee that baby is going to be immediately successful.

Denial reared its ugly head when I began to suspect that Infant Number Four was not nursing well. He was a sleepy baby, which certainly was not unusual for a newborn. I couldn't hear him swallowing very often, but surely it was because of all the background noise created by three older siblings. And, yes, his diapers weren't as wet as I'd like them to be, but they certainly weren't dry. There couldn't possibly be anything wrong with the way he was nursing. Okay, so he was completely rejecting my left breast, but Infant Number Three had done the same thing. Since my right breast was roughly the size of a basketball, there had to be enough milk in there to fully nourish my son.

Then, Pride stepped in. "Who, ME? A mother of FOUR EXCLUSIVELY BREASTFED babies, having trouble nursing my newest infant? That is preposterous." My husband's first gentle suggestion that we see a lactation nurse was met with immediate resistance. "You've got to be kidding. I KNOW WHAT I'M DOING...THIS IS MY FOURTH CHILD. How can I possibly show up at the hospital asking for help?" And yet, when my son was nine days old, there I stood, in the lactation office of the hospital where I'd given birth.

My first, embarrassed words to the sweet lady who came to greet me were more of an apology: "This is my fourth baby...I shouldn't have to be here!"   She smiled warmly and empathetically, and shared a story that immediately set me at ease.

"You know," she said, "one of our lactation nurses had her fourth baby, and she didn't even realize at first that the baby wasn't nursing properly.   Finally when he was a couple of months old, she brought him in so we could help her.   'I shouldn't be here…I'm a lactation nurse!' she said.   So, you see, it doesn't matter how many babies you've had.   Some babies need extra help learning how to nurse."

Having come to terms with being there, I handed my son over to the nurse so that she could weigh him.   My heart sank as I discovered that he had not even regained his birth weight. "Failure…I'm a failure," wafted through my perfectionist brain. "All right, let's see how he does," said the nurse.   In other words, "Bare your breast and let me stare at you while you attempt to nurse your baby."   I tried to act casual as I unhooked the flap of my nursing bra and attempted a successful latch-on.

The bottom line: my son was latching on poorly and had a faulty suckle.   He was pursing his little lips and sucking tightly on my nipple, his tongue arched and taut instead of open and curled around my areola.   The solution: basic training.   I was given a syringe, several tubes, a nipple shield (which I never did use), and a wondrous device called a Haberman feeder, which is a bottle with a special nipple that forces the infant to suckle properly in order to get the breastmilk out.   Daddy was commissioned to help with as many feedings as possible.   The reason?   His thumb was the largest available, and part of training was attaching a feeding tube to one's thumb, and pushing the baby's tongue down while administering the breastmilk from the syringe.

How long would this take? It all depended on how quickly my baby caught on. It could be days....or weeks...or even months. I had to make a decision then and there: how committed was I? My husband and I both agreed: if need be, we would do this until our son was six months old. If he hadn't learned by then, we'd give up.

From the moment we left the hospital with all our paraphernalia, I traded my womanhood for life as a Holstein. For along with all the tubes and gadgets, I carried with me a double-sided breast pump. Eight times a day I pumped, while my baby was fed either through a tube or with the Haberman feeder. After several days of this, I felt I needed a second trip to the lactation nurse, to make sure we were doing things properly. It was a different woman this time; equally sweet, but with hands smelling as though she had eaten an onion-laden hoagie for lunch and then slathered medical lotion on them. I couldn't wait to get away from that smell.

My life had become a blur of washing bottles and syringes, freezing breastmilk, and watching sadly over the hum of the breast pump as my son received his nourishment from his father. To be sure, it was a wonderful experience for my husband. And of course, I had my fair share of tube and bottle feedings as well. But my longing to simply curl up and nurse my son was at times overwhelming.

Then, one day, after only two weeks, my son latched onto my right breast and nursed. I was exuberant! Since he was still rejecting the left breast, I continued to pump milk from that side. I would have continued doing so indefinitely, if it weren't for the straightforward approach of my husband one afternoon. While watching me attempt a latch-on to my left breast, Eric suddenly reached over and said, "He needs to do this." He took his finger and formed a seal between my areola and the baby's lips. It worked! All of a sudden, the baby was nursing from the offensive left breast.

Until Spencer was weaned, I had to begin each feeding on the left; if I started on the right side, he wouldn't want anything at all from the other, unloved breast. It was no matter, though - lopsided breasts were a small price to pay for the ultimate success of our nursing experience.

Would I do it all over again? Absolutely. The benefits of nursing my son were worth the extra time and effort. Nothing beats the nutritional value of breastmilk. And nothing beats the sweetness of an infant at my breast.

Not even chocolate.

Mind Your Own Business

My firstborn son was sleeping peacefully in his infant seat as I began pushing the cart through the aisles of the grocery store. I had timed it just right: by the time I was finished shopping, it would be time for his next nursing. His tiny, two-month-old face kept distracting me as I hastened from produce to canned goods to pasta. Halfway through my venture, he stirred.

My heart sank as I watched his little eyes open. The grace period had ended. Within minutes he was wriggling, then grunting. By the time I reached the meat department, he was in a full-tilt wail. I felt my face flushing as I raced to get what I needed so that we could leave the store.

Then it happened. A woman, whose cart was in front of mine, clucked her tongue and said, "Feed that baby!"

Feed that baby? Had I actually heard her telling me to feed my baby? Did she think I was starving him so that I could get my shopping done? Or was she one of those people who assumes that every crying baby must be hungry? Perhaps she was so bothered by his crying that she felt an insuppressible need to say something irritating. Or maybe she simply had to let me know that I was an incompetent mother.

Did you ever have an overwhelming desire to tell a stranger to SHUT UP?

No, I didn't do it. But there are a few things I would have liked to say.

"And where might I do that, ma'am? Should I just stand over there by the chicken parts and whip out my breast? Or maybe I should take him into that disgusting bathroom and expose him to all sorts of germs just to keep him quiet."

Or maybe.....

"You obviously don't know anything about babies. My baby is on a three-hour feeding schedule and it is not time for him to nurse. I'm not going to screw up his schedule to appease you or anyone else."

Then again.....

"I have no intention of feeding my baby. I'm trying to see how many people I can annoy, so every time he dozes off I poke him so that he wakes up and screams. I take great delight in dealing with a screaming infant."

Or... "Shut up." Now, that would have been more to the point.

Of course I am hyperbolizing. Flinging a rude answer at a well-meaning but misguided stranger would not accomplish anything beyond a brief feeling of evil satisfaction. Society often seems clogged with folks who don't know how to mind their own business. I am sure the woman in the grocery store meant me no harm. Her ill-timed, insensitive comment was the last thing I needed at that stressful moment of new-mommyhood, but, in the larger scheme of things, it wasn't worth a second thought.

How, then, should we deal with unwelcome comments from outsiders? The best response will be tempered with tact and grace ("It's so hard when they cry, isn't it?"). Another option is to completely ignore the comment. It often seems like, when we are in public with our little ones, we have suddenly entered an open forum for comments on everything from our feeding choices to our disciplinary tactics, and even the size of our family. It is important that we are secure enough in the choices we have made to face these verbal onslaughts without getting our feathers ruffled. It really is nobody's business how we deal with a crying baby, whether our two-year-old is potty trained, or how many children we have ("My goodness, are these all YOURS?"). If we learn to take these comments with a grain of salt, we will be much more relaxed whenever they are flung our way.

Then again, on a really bad day, "SHUT UP" might serve us well.

Cloth Diaper Queen

I don't know how the idea first got into my head, but some time during my first pregnancy I decided that our baby was going to wear cloth diapers.

Notice: I said, "I decided," not, "WE decided." This was an executive decision made by the person who knew she would be in charge of at least ninety percent of the diaper changes. Having done my research, I had come to the conclusion that cloth diapers would be better for the environment and my baby's bottom, and slightly less expensive than disposables. Daddy-to-be merely shrugged and went along with the plan.

I was all smiles the day "Mr. Diaper" first arrived on my doorstep. He brought with him a wonderful, tall diaper pail and showed me how to insert the deodorant disk. (This was the Mercedes Benz of diaper pails; unlike the shrimpy varieties found in the stores, this one actually held an entire week of soiled diapers.) Mr. Diaper then lovingly demonstrated the proper folding of a cloth diaper, and the right way to insert it into the diaper cover. With his final instruction to call him when the baby arrived, he left, leaving behind a white, plastic bag filled with eighty tiny, cotton diapers.

Most hospitals, of course, do not use cloth diapers, and so for the first two days of his life, little Jonathan was destined to wear the offensive disposable variety. Once the first, sticky meconium poopies had been passed, I was eager to get his little bottom into the nice, soft diapers waiting for him at home. (Daddy, however, thought the disposable ones were more than acceptable.)

Truthfully, cloth diapers were not that much more work than disposables. When Jonathan needed a diaper change, I simply opened up the diaper cover, removed the diaper, threw it in the diaper pail, and stuck a new one back into the cover, which closed easily with Velcro. Of course, there was a slight propensity for leaking. Most of the time the diaper cover would catch the mess. I have a clear memory of standing in front of the bathroom sink at 4:00 in the morning, rinsing poopy out of a diaper cover, and grinning like a goon at my reflection in the mirror. "I love this," I murmured crazily. "I absolutely love this!" The scary part was – I was serious. Breastmilk poopies are not offensive, so it really didn't faze me to have to deal with a mess from time to time.

We found, of course, that it made more sense to use disposable diapers whenever we were out in public. Daddy enjoyed the switch, but I couldn't wait to get Jonathan back into his environmentally sound diapers. Try as he might, my husband could not get me to admit that disposable diapers were better. I was a Cloth Diaper Junkie. I had even won a contest run by my diaper service to come up with a name for their newsletter: my entry, "The Bottom Line," won me one free week of diaper service. How could I jump ship after having had such an honor bestowed upon me?

When Jonathan was nine weeks old, we packed up the car and headed to the Maryland shore for a week's vacation with my parents. Packed amidst our staggering load of newborn paraphernalia was a jumbo pack of disposable diapers. There was no way around it; Jonathan was going to have to spend an entire week wrapped in plastic.

Ocean breezes, walks on the beach, and no diaper covers to rinse – what a week! My husband was convinced that cloth diapers had been the worst idea I'd had in years, and he was sure that this vacation would change my mind about them. When we finally arrived home, there sat a fresh batch of cloth diapers, waiting for my eager hands to fold them. But wait –

my hands weren't quite so eager. In eight, short days I had become happily accustomed to the ease of disposable diapers. Of course, I couldn't possibly let Eric know. I was the Cloth Diaper Queen, and, true to my reign, I continued using the cloth diapers.

But – oh! How nice it was to pack three or four disposable diapers into the diaper bag for church on Sunday mornings! How delightful to change Jonathan's disposable diaper in a department store restroom! Was my eagerness showing? Was it obvious that I procrastinated every Monday when the fresh diapers arrived and I was supposed to fold them and stack them? Was that the trace of a victorious smile I saw dancing about the corners of Daddy's mouth?

Five months. It took five months to convert me. I called the diaper service and, after graciously declining further service, gleefully filled the top drawer of the changing table with Pampers. I had done my duty for the environment, and now it was time to take care of my own sanity.

Believe it or not, when I was pregnant with my second child, I once again decided to use cloth diapers. "You've got to be kidding," was Daddy's response. I was adamant. Yes, the disposables were more convenient, but we could use those later. I didn't want that tiny, newborn bottom to have anything except cotton rubbing against it.

This time, I lasted two months. Maggie was too voracious a pooper, and I was too tired a mommy-of-two, to deal with it any more. Jonathan was still in diapers when Maggie was born, so perhaps I could attribute the jumping-ship to diaper overload. At any rate, my cloth diaper regime ended once and for all. By the time I was pregnant for the third time, the thought never entered my mind. And when my fourth pregnancy rolled around, I couldn't even remember what a cloth diaper looked like.

Well, I take that back. They make great burpy pads, and even better dust cloths. I wish I still had a few lying around. Diaper service diapers are the "real thing;" you can't find the same quality of cloth diapers in any retail store. That's probably because nobody wants them.

It's a matter of preference, really, as well as temperament. If you are the patient, longsuffering sort who wants to use only "natural" things for your baby, then go ahead and try a diaper service. Mine was reliable and customer-oriented – a good experience overall. If, however, you tend to be high strung or would rather not spend extra time doing simple tasks, then save yourself some hassle. Start clipping coupons for disposable diapers, and stock up when there's a sale. In the long run, your baby's bottom won't really know the difference.

Don't you just hate it when your husband is right?

On Baby's Weight Gain and Doctors With An Attitude

"Not thriving."

There was no mistake: I had heard my pediatrician speak those dreadful words into his micro-cassette recorder. Minutes earlier I had asked him, "What about Jonathan's weight?" The doctor checked the chart, reading what I already knew: at nine months, Jonathan weighed sixteen pounds, eight ounces – exactly what he had weighed at six months. My little boy had not gained a single ounce in three months.

Weakly, I pointed out that Jonathan did seem to spit up a lot, but that in the past week or so it had seemed to diminish. The pediatrician dismissed it. He wanted Jonathan to have some tests right away.

Tests? My little boy needed tests? This was not how his nine-month check-up was supposed to turn out. Instead of receiving a glowing report of how big and fat my baby was growing, I watched as the nurse drew blood from Jonathan in order to check his white blood cell count. Since it was Friday, we had to wait until Monday to do further testing.

That night, Eric and I came to the conclusion that, surely, this had something to do with Jonathan's spitting up habit. Perhaps I had underplayed it to the doctor earlier that day; as a first-time mom, I really had no idea what amount of spitting up was considered "normal." We had noticed that whenever Jonathan ate solid finger foods in addition to the jarred baby food, he spit up less. Our immediate decision was to inundate him with table food. It could well be, we thought, that my approach to introducing foods had been much too conservative.   Jonathan's diet at that time still consisted of mostly pureed baby foods, along with some Cheerios, banana slices, and a few other "real" foods, in addition to still nursing three times a day. Could this be as simple as making a diet change?

Over the weekend, we changed Jonathan's diet to include everything from eggs to cheese to whole wheat bread - and we prayed for him. The spitting up virtually stopped. By the time Monday morning arrived, I was convinced that we had discovered the solution to Jonathan's weight gain problem. But there were still the tests to endure. Monday's wasn't difficult: another simple blood draw that only took a few minutes. When the results of both blood tests came back negative, our doctor informed us that Jonathan's lack of weight gain could be one of two things: an acid imbalance, or a nutritional problem due to vomiting. In order to leave no stone unturned, he sent us to the Vanderbilt Children's Clinic for more blood work and a urinalysis.

Despite the fact that Eric and I were convinced that Jonathan's problem was nutritional, having to go through further testing was emotionally draining. There is nothing quite like the helpless feeling of knowing that something may be wrong with your child. Jonathan was the love of our lives; we knew we would do anything we could for him.

At Vanderbilt, I watched as a nurse placed a plastic bag over Jonathan's penis, in order to catch some urine. That was painless enough, and now we merely had to wait for another doctor to arrive to do the final blood work.

The doctor and an intern soon arrived. After introducing herself, the doctor superciliously began to inform us that we were expected to leave during the blood test, and that afterward they would bring Jonathan out to us. In one of the most condescending tones I have ever heard, she said, "And YOU can be the 'good guy.'" I had had no intention of leaving my little boy during the test, and I was somewhat dazed as Eric escorted me into the hallway. Then, in an instant, I regained my composure, and felt the rage surging to the surface.

"I can't BELIEVE she asked us to leave!" I hissed in a much-too-loud stage whisper. "There was no reason I couldn't stay in there with him!"

"Shsh," was Eric's response.

"I will not be quiet!" Uh-oh, I was definitely out of control now. "She had no right to tell me to leave my baby alone in there! How does she think he feels for me to just LEAVE him in there?"

On and on I went until Eric finally calmed me down and ushered me into the waiting room. A few short minutes later, I got to be "the good guy" as Jonathan was brought to me, much more unscathed from the experience than I seemed to be.

Allow me to slightly digress in order to say that, should this situation have occurred in my life *now*, there is no way that I would have left Jonathan in the room. While it is imperative to usher relatives from rooms in which surgery or something equally serious is about to be administered, there was no reason to request our departure from the observance of a simple blood test. Not only that, but the condescending demeanor of the female doctor was highly offensive, and today I simply would not stand for it. She might as well have said, "Now, you little stay-at-home mommy, I know you don't have any clue about what I'm going to do to your son, and we wouldn't want you to faint dead away, would we? So you just go ahead and leave the room with your hubby, and I'll take care of it while you're gone, because after all, I'm a doctor, and you probably don't even have a college degree." At the very least, she should have respectfully asked us whether we preferred to stay or leave during the blood test.

If I were faced with this situation today, what would I say? "I'm sorry, but I don't ever leave my son with strangers. I really don't see any reason why I can't stay and observe this blood test; it's the third one he's had and I was there for the other two." And if the doctor refused to honor my request? I would take my child and leave. (Funny, I have yet to come across this supercilious attitude in any male doctors; but that, I am sure, is another story altogether.)

At any rate, the testing was complete, and we now had simply to wait for the results. They weren't long in coming, and to our relief – but not really to our surprise – they were negative. The conclusion? Jonathan had merely spit up his entire weight gain for the past three months. Did I feel like a failure? Absolutely. Especially when my father, without thinking, teased me over the phone by saying, "Why are you starving my grandson?" As the months passed, though, and I watched as Jonathan gained weight and developed into a healthy toddler, I realized that he had suffered no ill effects, and I was able to let go of my self-condemnation.

What have I learned? First of all, that it is very important to communicate clearly with the pediatrician. If I had described the extent to which Jonathan had been spitting up (it was everywhere; it was the color of whatever he had eaten most recently; it decorated almost every outfit in my closet), the testing may have been foregone altogether. Secondly, I have learned that, no matter how conscientious a mother I am, at times I will make mistakes, and it is imperative that I forgive myself in order to remain effective. And, of course, I've learned that it's perfectly all right for a nine-month-old to enjoy a peanut butter sandwich from time to time.

As for condescending, authoritative, professional women? I'm still working on that one.

The Sugarless Child

I admit it. Not only was I a first-time mommy – I was a Sugar Nazi. The baby book that was my second Bible had pounded into my head: "DO NOT GIVE A SINGLE OUNCE OF SUGAR TO ANY CHILD UNDER TWO!" Desiring to be the perfect mother, I made the decision to follow this advice to the letter, and never sully my under-two-year-old son with refined sugar.

Truly, there is much wisdom in this advice. First of all, there is no good reason to give ice cream to a seven-month-old, or to fill up baby's sippy cup with Coke at his first birthday party. Refined sugar fills baby up with calories that lack the nutrition he needs to grow and develop. Developing a "sweet tooth" early on will only make it harder for baby to enjoy more nutritious foods. And, of course, refined sugar wreaks havoc on baby's brand-new teeth. So, while it may be gratifying for adults to watch the blissful expression on a little one's face while he devours his first spoonfuls of chocolate cream pie, it does not ultimately benefit the child (and exactly who is it that we are supposed to be concerned about here, right?).

Having said that, I must hang my head at the extremes to which I took this stance against sugar. Jonathan did not start his finger-food days with Cheerios, like most other babies, but with fruit-sweetened, whole-grain "O-shaped" cereal that somewhat resembled guinea pig food. The cereal was so hard that I had to soak it in milk or water before handing it to my son. I also bought plain yogurt, into which I stirred fruit-only jellies and jams. Peanut butter remained exempt from my war against sugar. I couldn't bring myself to buy the organic, unsweetened stuff that needed to have the oil mixed into it before serving. Cookies, however, had to be fruit-sweetened. I am still amazed at what I was willing to pay for a box that contained only twelve "cookies." Of course, I wasn't eating any of them myself, since the sugar rules applied only to my son. I was going to do everything in my power to ensure that my son would have an essentially sugar-free babyhood.

Imagine my consternation when, upon picking Jonathan up from the church nursery one Sunday, I noticed a distinctly sweet, sugary smell emanating from his face. I sniffed him suspiciously.

"Eric!" I hissed. "Jonathan smells like a cookie. SOMEONE GAVE JONATHAN A COOKIE!!"

Husbands often fail to rise to the level of emotional response we expect from them, and my husband remained true to his sex: "Well, they didn't know." Clearly this was my own, personal battle.

The foundations of my sugar-free world severely shaken, I grappled with how to address the issue with the nursery staff. They were a wonderful, caring bunch, and I had no desire to offend anyone. Nevertheless, I had to make it clear that no further breach of the Sugar Law would be tolerated.

I wrote a letter. A ghastly, wacko-extremist-first-time-mommy letter, which accompanied Jonathan's diaper bag, was to become my nursery legacy. "Jonathan is not to have anything with sugar in it." That is the condensed version.

When we picked Jonathan up the following Sunday, a gentle-spirited man named Jack came forward apologetically. "I'm the one who gave him the animal cracker....I'm sorry." Feeling slightly like "Mommy Dearest," I assured him that there were no hard feelings. Nothing more was said about the letter, and Jonathan never again smelled like cookies.

The months passed. We were well into Jonathan's second year, and he had since "graduated" to the next class in the nursery. Eager to see his new room, I peeked in one Wednesday night when no one was there.

To my horror, attached to the wall above Jonathan's diaper bag hook was The Letter. The staff had moved it along with Jonathan up to Room Four. I couldn't erase the fact that, in my zeal, I had overreacted to a single animal cracker, which, if I am honest with myself, doesn't even fit into the "cookie" category. Now, my own handwriting stared back at me from the nursery wall: "See how neurotic you are? Your words go before you for all to see. Your son is marked."

You may think that, at that point, I rushed home and fed Jonathan a few cupcakes. On the contrary, I held out until his second birthday, on which he enjoyed his first chocolate cake and vanilla ice cream. But something had snapped, and the "snapping" was to manifest itself in the rearing of my three subsequent children.

You see, none of them have had to wait until their second birthdays to experience chocolate or ice cream...or even the dreaded animal crackers. Somewhere in the unconscious recesses of my frenetic mind, the thought occurred to me that Jonathan had suffered absolutely no ill effects from the illegal animal cracker. And, besides...animal crackers are cheap and travel nicely in little plastic baggies.

Of course I still strongly believe in holding off as long as possible on sweets. The days of fructose cookies are long gone, though, and my pantry proudly displays Cheerios, Kix, and two-pound bags of animal crackers for my toddler. I remain conservative in my approach to food-introduction, but I like to think that I am much more relaxed now.

The ultimate test came when my youngest was ten months old. I had just left him in his very baby-proofed room while I tended to another task. Jonathan, whom I had sent to keep an eye on the baby, suddenly came running back down the hallway, calling my name in a panicked voice.

"Mommy!" He was close to tears. "Mommy! Spencer has chocolate."

Chocolate? How could he have chocolate? I remained calm as I hastened to the baby's room. Upon opening the door, I discovered my little guy lying contentedly on the floor beside a small, heart-shaped box. In his mouth was a slowly melting chocolate, which had left its mark all over his face and the carpet as well. I removed the chocolate from his mouth (he was not too pleased) and cleaned up the mess.

Unlike seven years earlier, my world did not fall apart. I did not have Spencer's stomach pumped or throw all the remaining chocolates down the garbage disposal in protest (what a horrible waste of chocolate that would have been). If anything, I was proud of myself for showing restraint and keeping things in perspective. Adding children to the nest seems to have that effect. It's not that the novelty has worn off, but rather that the high-strung protectiveness has.

Displaying wisdom and common sense without frenzy is my ultimate character goal. Chocolate, anyone?

Poop

My husband has an old, white undershirt with a tan stain on the front. The stain, which is over nine years old, still elicits goofy smiles from him, as he points to it and coos, "This is from Jonathan!"

Yes, it's a poopy stain. My husband waxes nostalgic over an old poopy stain.

Mind you, the stain was caused by a breastmilk poopy, which is far less offensive than the more mature, I'm-eating-solids-now kind. In my husband's defense, the nostalgia didn't stem from the poop itself, but from the sweet memory attached to it. When Jonathan was very tiny, Eric used to give him his morning feeding of bottled breastmilk. After warming the bottle, he would situate himself on the rocking chair in Jonathan's room, and in the gentle, morning light he would prop the baby up against his knees and feed him. Jonathan never did take very well to the bottle, and never drank more than an ounce or two. As a result, I always had to breastfeed him again in two hours. It was really fine, though, since the little "mini-feeding" afforded me some extra sleep, and gave Eric precious time with his little boy.

It was during one of these morning feedings that Jonathan suddenly decided to expel a larger-than-usual amount of poop into his diaper. Before Daddy had a chance to lift him up, Jonathan's diaper had begun to leak onto his tee shirt. Poopy stains can be rather obstinate, and this one was no exception. Through the years, the stain has remained on the shirt, and it still brings a smile to Eric's face.

Nobody ever tells you, before you start your family, how much a part of your life poopy will become. Single people grimace and gag as new moms and dads chatter nonchalantly about the latest poop escapades in their lives. Women with children don't hesitate to discuss their offspring's bodily functions over lunch. Poop is so much a part of life as a parent, in fact, that after a while one hardly gives it a second thought.

Isn't that scary?

When Jonathan was eighteen months old, I threw a Christmas party for some friends. The candles were lit, the table was spread, and I was fluttering about like the frenetic hostess I always am. Suddenly, I noticed some small, brownish objects under the Christmas tree. Since Jonathan was standing very near the tree, it took me no time at all to discern what the brown objects were, although my initial reaction was one of denial. "No! Jonathan did NOT just poop under the tree in front of all my guests!"

It wasn't just any poop – it was a "raisin poop." All of my children have experienced the phenomenon of a raisin poop, although Jonathan's were the most alarming. You see, when a small child eats a raisin, it doesn't get chewed very much, so when it enters the body it rehydrates and comes out the other end all plump and juicy. A recycled grape, if you will.

So, there were several of these "recycled grapes" lying on the carpet under my Christmas tree. Obviously they had rolled out of Jonathan's diaper, down his pants leg, and onto the floor. My guests found this highly amusing. Since I didn't think it would have been in good taste to explain the raisin poop thing to them, I quietly cleaned up the mess, changed Jonathan's diaper, and went on with the evening.

Then, of course, there is the experience of jet-propelled poopies, seen most often in very young babies. Maggie was notorious for excreting so much poopy that it would go up the back of her diaper and keep on traveling north, sometimes almost reaching the back of her neck. I had never seen anything like it. I should have been prepared for it, though, after watching her blast the bedroom wall with a poopy at the tender age of two weeks. In the few seconds it had taken me to remove her diaper and slip another one under her bottom, she had taken aim and fired. I remember staring at the streak on the wall in disbelief.

Disbelief soon gives way to matter-of-factness. Poop on little socks that kick during diaper changes; poop on my pants where the baby was sitting; poop on chubby fingers that reached down before I had had a chance to wipe; poop on the changing table; poop in the car seat; poop everywhere.

Then of course, there's the opposite of poop everywhere, which is poop nowhere. Rachel, my third blessing, decided to stop pooping altogether when she was approaching six months. Days would go by without so much as a speck in her diaper, and when she finally was able to relieve herself, the result would resemble nothing more than large apple seeds. As though I had not had enough poop in my life, I was now desperate to see some in her diaper. Poop had become such an integral part of my daily existence that now it seemed I could not function without it.

The pediatrician informed me that the lack of poop was due to the fact that Rachel wasn't getting enough calories, and it was time to introduce solids. After a week or two on cereal, Rachel's caloric intake obviously righted itself, and her diapers were once again filled with ever-present poopy, albeit of the new, fragrant variety. No matter – I was happy to have a pooping daughter once again.

Just when you think you've had it with poop, your child moves from the diaper phase to the potty-training phase. Poopy is transformed from something that needs to be discarded into something that needs to be applauded. When Jonathan finally pooped in his potty-chair for the first time, I whipped out my camera.

Yes, I took a picture of his poop.

Well, why not? Poop was so much a part of our lives, why not capture it on film? Of course, I do think that that was one photo my parents weren't too excited about receiving in the mail. It had been too many years since their lives had been poopy-filled.

I am sure that at some point of my life I will no longer be under the influence of poop. I would say that I dream of the free-from-poopy lifestyle, except that I really can't remember what that means. Living my life up-to-the-elbows in poop is all I've known for many years. What will my girlfriends and I talk about? What excuse will I have to wash my hands? What new, refreshing scents will my nose detect? It is a mystery to me.

I take comfort in the thought that I am not alone. Surely there are women all over the earth who spend their days with poop in all its forms, and who think nothing of it. It is an inherent part of motherhood, yes? And we, sisters on the journey, have poop as our ultimate common bond. It transcends race, religion, parenting styles, and personality types. And when we have finally passed the baton to those who are younger and just starting out on the path of parenthood, we will pass along also the baby wipes, toilet paper, and Lysol disinfectant.

We will finally, boldly step into a life free of poop.

Milestones

On Thumb-sucking

I think thumb-suckers are cute.

One of the first, great loves of my life was my sister Jamie. Born when I was three and a half years old, she was, for several years, truly my "little" sister. And one of her most endearing qualities was the fact that she sucked her thumb. I can still see her cherubic face – those soft, "vanilla" cheeks, the thick, dark locks, and the sweetly curled fist propped deftly against her mouth. Except for the early morning hours when her incessant sucking noises annoyed me from the adjacent bedroom, I loved her thumb-sucking. As she started to outgrow her habit, I would ask her to put her thumb in her mouth for a minute, so that I could momentarily revel in her cute-ness. When she finally got to the point at which she would no longer comply, I had to accept the fact that my "baby" sister wasn't very babyish anymore.

Perhaps my love for my sister explains my penchant for thumb-suckers. Linus, for instance, has always been my favorite Peanuts character. He is not only the wisest in the bunch, but the cutest as well – all on account of that firmly implanted thumb.

It was no small joy, then, when my firstborn turned out to be a thumb-sucker. After being able for some time to find his tiny thumb while lying on his belly, he surprised me at eleven weeks by sticking it in his mouth while sitting in his infant seat. The next night he was able to get himself back to sleep without having to be nursed – because he had found, instead, a beloved thumb.

"Thummie," as we have always called it, became more and more prominent in his little life. By the time Jonathan turned one, Thummie and Blankie were each an integral part of his days – and nights. I never had a problem with it – after all, I had made the decision prior to his birth that he would not be a pacifier baby. Honestly, the thought of sticking a plastic plug in his mouth to get him to sleep revolted me. I did use a pacifier during the early weeks when he needed an extra suck or two, but there was no way that I was going to let him get addicted to it.

I much preferred the sweet "addiction" of his own thumb.

Thumb-suckers, you see, don't wake their mommies in the middle of the night because their sucking source has fallen on the dark floor underneath the crib. Thumb-suckers don't grow horrible, crusty rashes on their faces from plastic-entrapped saliva. And thumb-suckers actually take their thumbs out of their mouths to play instead of sitting there with their faces obscured by a multi-colored plug. Have you ever seen a three-year-old sporting a gigantic, toddler-sized plug in his mouth? I have – and it wasn't pretty.

Give me a thumb-sucker any day.

Dentists may scoff, "He's got to stop that soon…he'll mess up his mouth." There may be some truth to that, as evidenced by my sister's orthodontic problems. Jonathan, though, was through with his thumb by the time he was five, and there was no damage to his mouth or teeth. I admit – I felt somewhat vindicated. Jonathan was able to enjoy years of self-comfort, and I was able to enjoy the breathtaking sweetness of my little, blond thumb-sucker.

There is something indescribably precious about kissing the warm, little corner of a sleeping mouth from which a thumb has half-emerged. Sometimes the kiss evokes the involuntary response of the mouth's sucking the thumb back into its place;

other times, the thumb remains motionless in sleep – or else it slides gently down the velvety cheek, onto the pillow.

I am a complete goner for thumb-suckers.

My second-born never sucked on anything. My third-born was a finger-sucker (not nearly as cute as thumb-sucking, but equally convenient in the middle of the night.) I longed for the days of Thummie and Blankie.

Along came Spencer. To my delight – to my rapture – he is a thumb-sucker! It began casually enough: at times it seemed he was only half-sucking his thumb. It soon became a strong part of his persona, and after awhile it included a Blankie as well. Another Blond Boy with Thummie and Blankie – it was too good to be true!

And so, I continue to sing the praises of thumb-sucking. Once again I have sleeping thummie-lips to kiss, heart-melting thummie-photographs to shoot, and a wet, wrinkled little thummie to wipe off when it's time to eat lunch.

"Oh, the thumb-sucker's thumb is wrinkled and wet,
And withered, and white as the snow,
But the taste of a thumb is the sweetest taste yet –
As only we thumb-suckers know."   ---Shel Silverstein[1]

Potty Training Blues

I hate potty-chairs.

Admittedly, I didn't always feel that way. The first time around, potty training was like a badge of honor - a sign of effective motherhood. Jonathan's potty-chair might as well have been a throne. Despite the fact that my early attempts at training him were ultimately unsuccessful, the potty-chair maintained its place of honor and respect in the bathroom. Memories of the first successful landing of a poopy in the pot kept the fire going, so to speak.

Still, it wasn't until Jonathan was almost three years old that I came upon the potty training wisdom that enabled me to train him in only three days.

Three days. I'm not kidding!

The advice was simple and straightforward, and it came from the pages of one of Dr. John Rosemond's parenting books. Here is my paraphrase: "You are in charge of potty-training. Your child is not." Think about it - if we waited for our children to tell us that they were ready to eat vegetables, they'd never eat them. If we waited for our children to tell us when they wanted to see the pediatrician, they'd be living doctor-free lives. Why would we want to wait for them to tell *us* when they wanted to use a potty-chair? Think of the convenience of a diaper: squat where you are and go. Some hapless grown-up will clean up the mess later. What self-respecting toddler would want to change the system?

And so, with renewed vigor, I got rid of Jonathan's diapers once and for all, and put him into cloth training pants. Following Dr. Rosemond's advice, I set a timer. When the bell rang, it was potty time. No power struggle between mom and child. No begging him to sit down and pee on command. And no bribes of endless rewards for proper excrement habits (why build a sense of self-importance around the act of pooping?). Once the bell rang, it was time to sit down. Period. If nothing happened after ten or fifteen minutes, we simply pulled up the pants and waited until the next timer bell rang. If an accident occurred in between potty times, it was cleaned up without fuss.

It's amazing how efficiently something can be accomplished when Mom actually takes charge.

Girls, of course, are different. Both of my daughters were ready to be trained before their second birthdays. It's funny, though, how little girls, despite their early readiness, tend to "leak" more than boys do. Even though Maggie and Rachel were both wearing regular panties by the time they turned two, the panties often needed to be changed because of "drippies." This was the antithesis of my experience with Jonathan, who, once he was trained, never had a single accident. I often found myself wondering why in the world I had been so eager to move first Maggie, then Rachel, out of the diaper stage. Diapers were a lot less of a hassle than constantly moist, size 2T underwear!

Rachel took the challenge even further by requiring constant trips to the bathroom. No matter if she had used the bathroom before we left for a restaurant – when we arrived, she would announce, "Mommy, I have to go pee-pee." And this after a lapse of only twenty or thirty minutes! It was hard to hide my incredulity.

"Rachel, *you just went pee-pee twenty minutes ago.* How can you possibly need to go again?"

Sure enough, she would produce an entire toilet-bowlful of urine. Not to be caught off-guard a second time, I would look her in the eyes and ask, "Are you sure you are finished? Did you let *all* the pee-pee out this time?" I had no intention of letting her out of that bathroom stall until I was convinced that her pea-sized bladder was empty.

Public bathrooms are, in my opinion, the worst possible part of potty training. It's bad enough toting a freshly trained toddler around without really feeling all that secure about his bathroom habits. Taking that little person into a disgusting, germ-laden bathroom and trying to keep his little hands from touching anything while simultaneously assisting him in relieving himself is enough to make me want to simply stay home. It's easier on daddies of little boys, of course. Waltzing up to a urinal, holding up a too-short boy to help him aim, and pulling up a little pair of pants is a lot easier than lining a revolting toilet seat with paper and keeping a small girl from touching the seat or falling in.

For some unexplained reason, though, I always seemed to get stuck with Jonathan when he had to poop.

"Jill, the stalls in the men's room are really gross. I can't take him in there – I just can't!" Yeah, right. And the stalls in the women's room are fresh as daisies? Anyway, arguing seemed futile, and also put little Jonathan at risk of pooping in his pants. So into the ladies' room he would go. I derived great pleasure, though, whenever Eric would return from an outing with Jonathan and inform me that Jonathan had had to poop while they were out. It was quite tempting to say, "Oh? And did you take him to the ladies' room?"

So here I am, on the brink of training Child Number Four. And all I can come up with is: I hate potty-chairs. I've been through it – the pull-ups, the M-and-M's, the urine all over my lap. I know it's time to begin and I know just what to do. I simply don't want to do it!

How bad would it be, really, if Spencer wore diapers until he was old enough to train himself? He's such a little guy – I'm sure the diapers will still fit him a couple of years from now. Sure, it was awfully cute when he sat down on his brand-new potty-chair and pretended to go pee-pee and flush it. It was even (marginally) cute when he took his diaper off and put his little shorts back on, without telling me. But those soaking wet shorts didn't do much to inspire me to begin the training process. I felt the incredible weight of "here we go again."

Yes, the charm has worn off. But the need to get the job done hasn't gone away. I may groan and complain and drag my feet, but in the end I'll take charge and get my little guy potty-trained. It's the right thing to do, and it doesn't matter how I feel about it. It just helps, somehow, to get it off my chest.

In the meantime, if anyone knows of a free potty-training service – I'm all ears!

Bedwetters Don't Stink

Commercials for children's disposable, absorbent underwear anger me. In order to sell the product, bedwetting is portrayed as the ultimate social downfall of a child; the epitome of personal shame. "Buy this for your child, and he will no longer feel less than sub-human!"

I am the proud mother of two bedwetters. And, unequivocally, I can say that neither one has felt ashamed or insecure about it. Why? Because I've never made a big deal about it.

When Maggie was three and still wearing Pull-ups each night, I threw it out to her doctor. (I pause here to point out that it is a delicate art, indeed, to ask questions about a child's development while the child is sitting there, all ears.)

"Was anyone else in your family a bedwetter?" was the expected question that followed.

Funny he should ask. I have vivid memories of standing on the commode each morning before nursery school while my mother wiped the bottom half of me down with a warm, soapy washcloth. I wet the bed every night, in the days before disposable training pants. I still remember the feeling of the soaking wet slacks in which I had once fallen asleep. And I can still hear my mother saying, "We have to wipe you off so you don't smell."

I must have taken that fear of stinking with me each day to nursery school, until finally one day it roared to the surface. It was nap time, and as I lay quietly on my towel (we didn't have fancy, padded mats in those days), one of the teachers walked by and said to another teacher, "Something smells."

Of course, I assumed she meant me.

I began to cry. Mommy was right......I was stinky! The teachers asked me what was wrong. I wouldn't tell them. They called my mother to come and get me. While I was waiting for her, I sat on a wooden chair, crying, surrounded by concerned classmates. I would not tell them why I was crying. When my mother arrived, I would not tell her why I was crying, either.

I was too ashamed.

When we arrived at home a few minutes later, I immediately stopped crying and began to play. My mother was angry – she thought I had pretended to be sick so that she would bring me home. Little did she know that my world had fallen apart because she had unwittingly taught me to believe that bedwetting made me stinky, and that now my teachers knew about it.

When I was five, I was prescribed a small, red, triangular pill that helped me stop wetting the bed. Though it doesn't work for all children, it worked for me. That was a lifetime ago.

Despite my personal success with the drug (whatever it may have been), I wasn't interested in medicating my daughter. As an alternative, my doctor told me about the "Wee Alarm," which wakes children up whenever they start to urinate at night, until they are conditioned not to do so. It was intriguing, but too expensive to consider. Next option? Let her outgrow it.

In the meantime, Daughter Number Two was showing the same propensity for nocturnal wetness. Training pants for two were a part of our monthly budget that we weren't too thrilled about. Yet, we remained casual about the bedwetting, only requiring that the girls bring down their wet training pants each morning to throw them in the garbage.

We tried limiting drinks in the evening. We tried putting regular panties on them so that they wouldn't be so comfortable when they wet themselves. We even tried waking the girls up at night to take them to the toilet. "Do this for three months," the doctor said, "and I guarantee you they'll be dry."

It was just too stressful to deal with. We gave up. They both kept wetting the bed.

By now we had a newborn. I seriously feared that the cost of training pants *and* diapers would wipe us out. Maggie turned five. Surely at least SHE would soon be dry.

No such luck.

My mother, every so often, would attempt to encourage me with success stories: "You know, I was just talking to your cousin Jodi. She said that her Kevin was a bedwetter until he was five or so, and he just stopped wetting the bed on his own. One day she said that, all of a sudden, she realized that she couldn't remember the last time he'd been wet. See? It'll happen!"

Instead of feeling encouraged, I felt cynical. Not notice that the wetting had stopped? Give me a break.

Maggie turned six. Although once in a while she would surprise us all with a dry night, this only occurred once a month or less. Rachel, who was several months away from turning five, was soaking wet each morning. I came to the conclusion that, while Maggie did seem to be tapering off a bit, Rachel was still wetting herself at least three times each night. Both girls continued to take their "stinkies" downstairs each morning and throw them in the garbage (except for the days when the offensive objects were left in various and sundry other places, such as the bathroom floor, the closet, or the upstairs hallway, in full view of any visitor that might chance to grace our front door).

Never once did we shame them for being wet. Never once did they dissolve in tears because they had once again awakened to a wet pair of training pants.

Then, one day, I noticed a dry pair of training pants lying on the bedroom floor. "Maggie," I said, "Why is that Pull-up lying there?"

"Oh," said Maggie, ever so casually. "It's been dry, so I keep wearing the same one."

Huh?

"It's been DRY? For how long?" I was beyond incredulous.

"Oh, I don't know. Several days."

The next day, Daddy asked her the same question about the dry training pants.

"Well, I've been wearing this one, but it's starting to get stinky from wearing it every night, so I'm going to get a new one," was her response.

And how many days had she worn the first pair? "Oh, six." Another very casual reply.

That night I asked her if she'd like to wear regular panties to bed. She glowed, beamed, grinned as she ran to her room to put them on.

What blessed me most of all was Maggie's reason for being so quiet about her new "achievement:" She didn't want Rachel to feel badly. Maggie could have – should have – done back flips and cartwheels and set off a hundred fireworks. Instead, she deferred her celebration to the honoring of her little sister.

Was Rachel fazed? Not really. But I'm not surprised; after all, we have never made a big deal about wetting the bed. To her, it doesn't make much difference whether or not she still wears training pants each night.

And I think that is exactly as it should be.

Milestones

"You mean, he's not walking yet? And.... how old did you say he was?"

How does a new mommy keep her cool when faced with a question like this? Captive as we are to a society steeped in "keeping up with the Joneses," it is difficult to refrain from a similar mindset when it comes to our children.

Babies do not come into this world with owner's manuals and pre-determined schedules. Their bottoms are not stamped with "change by" dates; there is no toll-free number to call when there's a technical problem. Yet despite the assurances of modern child-care books that the range of "normal" for milestones is rather wide, we somehow expect our babies to develop according to some factory-determined timetable.

My firstborn was not walking at twelve months. To be honest, I wasn't overly concerned, since he had been cruising well for some time. When he finally took his first steps at thirteen and a half months, I was overjoyed. A couple of weeks later, Jonathan was toddling about on the Maryland shore where we were spending the week with my parents. As I lazily watched him playing in the shallow waves with his daddy, I suddenly noticed another little boy who looked about the same age. To my disdain, I saw that this OTHER little boy – this usurper of my attention – was able to stand up all by himself from a sitting position. Jonathan was not yet able to do that. I was bothered. Actually, I was beyond bothered. I wanted that smarmy mother to grab her son and head back to their condo.

Minutes earlier I had been luxuriating in Jonathan's delightful, babyish antics. Now I was nothing more than a jealous mom, wishing her son had climbed the achievement ladder as quickly as the next tyke. What had happened to me?

The moment passed; the season passed. Jonathan learned to stand up on his own – and to do everything else that a healthy little boy needs to do. The fact that his speech development was a little slow didn't bother me too much for two reasons. First of all, he was a boy, and everybody knows that boys develop more slowly than girls. Secondly, Jonathan was nothing short of a genius. He could name all his colors and identify a Mozart symphony at the age of two. Oh, yes, the days of worrying about trifles like standing and walking were over. We were fast headed toward Harvard.

"Oh, your three-year-old is having trouble learning her colors? Don't worry, she'll learn them in time. Oh, my Jonathan? Why, yes, he knows ALL his colors, including magenta and fuchsia."

Well, I didn't actually SAY anything like that – but I certainly thought it to myself.

Enter child number two. If Jonathan was a genius, then Maggie was certainly a child prodigy. She started talking at ten months, and never stopped. By eighteen months she was speaking in full sentences. Since she had walked at twelve months, I had no cause to fret over gross motor skills. Yes, I was on top of the world with this one! By the age of three she was sitting at the piano and picking out melodies by ear. If Jonathan was headed for Harvard, then Maggie was definitely headed for Julliard.

It's funny how nobody complains of a child doing something "too soon." We tend to wear our children's developmental achievements like badges. This can easily backfire if a subsequent child does not progress as quickly.

Rachel was my subsequent child. Born when Maggie was just seventeen months old, Rachel spent a lot of time lying in her bouncy seat, watching the chaos unfolding around her. At six months, she was not sitting. In fact, she didn't even roll over from her back to her belly until then. At eight months she could sit well. She took her first steps at thirteen and a half months, and at sixteen months was only saying a handful of words. The only thing she did early was cutting teeth – her first two had sprouted at five months.

"Rachel? No, she's not talking yet. Well, (nervous chuckle) you know what they say about third-borns. There's so much going on that there's no need to talk. She's just....absorbing."

Yes, but how did I REALLY feel? Was I capable of withholding comparison between my two daughters? Because it is severely damaging to a child's self esteem if he is made to feel that he is inferior to his siblings, I knew that I needed to rise above my frustration in order to affirm Rachel for who she was.

She rose to the occasion. Before her second birthday she knew all her colors and could identify the numbers one through nine by sight. She was also speaking in sentences and using the potty. And at the age of three she, too, was playing melodies by ear on the piano.

And then came Spencer.

Our hearts were captured from the moment we first saw his face. We brought him home to an apartment filled with doting siblings. No baby in the history of mankind has ever been more loved, coddled, and absolutely spoiled with attention. Every whimper was met with a kiss; every little sound was applauded; every need, real or perceived, was met by an eager brother or sister. Spencer didn't have to do a thing.

So, Spencer didn't do anything.

At fourth months he was having trouble keeping his head up while lying on his belly. It occurred to me that I had kept him in his bouncy seat too much. At eight months he finally sat up by himself, but complained about it (why sit up when there are five sets of arms in which to be held?). Instead of walking at thirteen months, he crawled on all fours. By sixteen months he was walking, but had yet to speak a single word. Shortly before his second birthday, Spencer's speech had developed into an elaborate language of which, aside from a dozen or so clear words, we understood nothing.

In the midst of his sluggish development, though, there emerged an unmistakable talent: Spencer had an incredible ear for music. His "singing" began at sixteen months as a random series of breathy pitches. By the time he was twenty months old, he was humming melodies with nearly perfect accuracy. Gradually, some of these melodies grew "words," which could be roughly translated into English lyrics. His ability to match pitch was remarkable.

Despite having a complete disregard for any "timetable" I may have wished him to follow, Spencer proved that his talents were there – as much a part of him as his hazel eyes and wispy, blonde hair. In each child has been planted, by Divine design, the gifts and talents unique to him. By relaxing and allowing our children to grow at their own pace, we will have the joy of watching these gifts unfold.

Four children – four unique development stories. I would venture to say that my children are as "normal" as can be. It may have taken me four tries to finally stop riding the "my-baby-is-farther-along-than-your-baby" train, but I take great comfort in knowing that I can at least pass along the wisdom I have gleaned. My children are neither prodigies nor geniuses.

They are beautiful, lovable, endlessly interesting little people who fill my life with joy.

And if one of them does something astonishing – well, you must forgive me if I brag a little. After all, nobody's perfect.

In The Life of a Mom

Mommy Meltdown

Once again, it happened when I least expected it. It was Friday.....not bad as far as days-of-the-week go. Breakfast was finished, the sun was shining, the first load of laundry was in the washer. The day held promise; Jonathan was engrossed in identifying a specific wildflower he had found in a vacant lot and the girls were entertaining their baby brother.

I don't know what snapped, but something did.

The girls suddenly decided that neither of them was interested in babysitting anymore, and Jonathan grew tired of our wildflower study and asked if he could go play. I felt the light inside of me flicker out; that tiny, almost imperceptible "pop" in my spirit, as if something had died, or at least run out of battery power. Suddenly, I didn't care about wildflowers, baby care, sunshine, or being a mom.

It was a meltdown.

I hung in there for a few more minutes, carefully pressing one of the wildflower blooms between the pages of a dictionary. Then, blankly, I took sweaty, cranky little Spencer upstairs to play in his bedroom until lunch time. I lay on the floor while he crawled around and clawed at my face and pulled all the clothing out of his bottom drawer. I didn't care......I was tired and it wasn't even noon.

Lunch was a series of "no's" and "will you stop that's;" I barely had the energy to finish cleaning up the kitchen afterward. Spencer's 1:00 nap seemed miles away. When it finally arrived, it afforded me no relief. My productivity was gone. The laundry stalled. My bed was unmade. I plopped onto the sofa to read Mary Luke's A Crown For Elizabeth.

Interesting thing, being a queen. You could have a baby and hand it over to an entire squadron of nursemaids and ladies-in-waiting, visiting it at your leisure. When Elizabeth was born, she was given an entire house to live in, along with her own private staff. Her mother, Anne Boleyn, occasionally graced her with a visit. That's not what I really wanted, though. After all, Anne Boleyn lost her head three years after Elizabeth's birth.

It happens to all of us, and affects each of us differently: the I'm-Totally-Burned-Out-And-Don't-Want-To-Be-A-Mom-Today syndrome. The smallest thing may set it off – like my son's sudden change of heart about the wildflowers – but it is more than likely the cumulative result of not allowing ourselves enough time to get away and refresh ourselves. As I write, I ask myself, when *is* the last time I got away by myself? And I cannot answer, unless I include this morning's trip to the grocery store.

I am completely devoted to my children; there is nothing I desire more than staying at home to raise them. My greatest joy is derived from the sweet, daily interface I have with each of them. Yet, to be true to myself, I need to recognize that I am a woman of energy, talent, and outside interests. If I do not take some time to revel in my other passions, I will eventually implode: meltdown. And there are thousands of other stay-at-home moms who are just like me.

Once I have melted down, I have nothing left to give. It's "go play" instead of "come here and I'll read you a story," and "Mommy's resting" instead of "What do you need?" The smallest task seems insurmountable. The more I push the children away, the worse I feel, and the worse I feel, the more I push them away. My one hope on days like this is that my husband will rise to his Prince Charming status and rescue me!

And so, on this particular Friday, I sent him an email: "I am soooooooooo irritable! I think I am really tired. I wish I could sleep. Even Spencer is driving me totally, totally, totally crazy. The weather is SO DELIGHTFUL, and I feel like a fuzz-head. WHAT IS WRONG WITH ME??? I wish I could spend the day with you. With no obligations....no children around, no laundry, no dirty bathroom to clean, no wasps to kill, no bloody foreheads to wipe, no whining to quell, no diapers to change, no dishwasher to stack, no lunch to make, no questions to answer, no phone to ignore, no articles to write, no orders to bark, NO NOTHING. "

My Meltdown Friday had a happy ending. Being the loving, sensitive man he is, my husband immediately discerned that I was burned out. He brought barbecue sandwiches home for supper, then shooed me out of the kitchen while he cleaned up afterward. I took a nice, cool shower while he tucked the children in bed, and then he and I spent a quiet, romantic evening chatting by candlelight. This morning, I woke up smiling.

The smiles won't last, though, unless I make a decided effort to give myself regular breaks. A quiet afternoon at the library; coffee with a friend; meandering through the aisles of Wal-Mart, looking for sales: making time for things like this makes all the difference in my day-to-day life.

What are you doing to avoid meltdown?

Ice Storm

"You're going to San Francisco for four days and leaving me alone with Jonathan?"

I made no excuse for being incredulous. Perhaps it was a normal occurrence for other families - as much a part of life as receiving the Sunday paper or making a weekly trip to the grocery store. For me, though, being left behind while my husband was out of town on business was nearly traumatic. For one thing, I was six months pregnant, and wallowing in the hormonal upheavals of my state of being. Besides that, I was terribly afraid of being alone in the dark at night. My twenty-month-old son wasn't able to do much to alleviate that.

How could Eric leave me?

Apparently, it wasn't too much of a struggle for him. After all, he was leaving the gloomy cold of a Nashville February for the balmy warmth of northern California. Any tears that were shed over our parting were mine alone.

The freezing rain was just starting as Eric's plane took off. Later, as I served Jonathan his spaghetti and tried not to feel the emptiness of Eric's absence, I was unaware of the treacherous, crystalline world that had developed outside my windows. The doors were locked, the television was on (normally an enemy, the television became my best ally whenever Eric was away), and I had no intention of going anywhere.

It was probably somewhere between six and seven o'clock in the evening. I was chatting on the phone long-distance with my sister, with one eye on Jonathan, who was standing in front of the television.

Suddenly, everything went black. Jonathan screamed.

What a horrible time for a power outage! The sudden darkness and silence would have been unbearable if it weren't for my sister's voice on the other end of the line. I couldn't let my own fear of the dark hinder me from calming my terrified toddler.

"Jamie, will you please stay on the line while I run and get a candle?"

While my obliging sister, who was well acquainted with my neuroses, waited, I ran into the darkness of my bedroom and groped through my closet until I found the large pillar candle I was looking for. Knowing that my sister was still on the phone helped to quell my unreasonable fear. Soon Jonathan and I were basking in the glow of candlelight, and I was able to release Jamie from her long-distance vigil. Surely the lights would come back on within the hour.

The lights didn't come back on.

As the evening wore on and the house grew colder, I became more worried. Jonathan's bedtime approached, and I knew I couldn't let him sleep in his cold bedroom. I decided to pull out the sofa bed so that we could sleep there together.

Now, by mentioning the fact that there was a fireplace right there in the living room, I may be setting my readers up for a premature sigh of relief. "Oh, a fireplace! That would keep you nice and warm all night." Indeed, it would have.... if I had known how to start a fire. Actually, the only fuel I had on hand was a stack of three "Dura-flame" logs, each of which was supposed to last for two hours. I decided to time the burning of the logs throughout the night.

I hadn't realized until that night that "Dura-flame" logs do not produce any heat.

Around 11:00, Eric called from sunny California: "How are you, Sweetie?"

"How am I? The electricity went off about four hours ago and it hasn't come back on yet and I'm freezing!"

Although slightly worried, Eric was convinced that the electricity would soon be restored. I imagine it was rather difficult for him to empathize. It was in the low seventies in San Francisco.

The next morning, the electricity was still off. The water heater had maintained enough hot water for me to take a warm shower in a very cold bathroom. I decided that the best thing to do would be to leave the house and find a nice, warm place to eat breakfast. So, I bundled Jonathan into the car and we headed to Cracker Barrel.

Signs of power loss and tree damage were evident as we drove along. Ironically, the ice that had caused such devastation (which was extensive, as I later learned), had already melted, and the temperature was in the forties. Imagine my relief when I discovered that Cracker Barrel was up and running and open for business. The place was packed.

I had never been so grateful for a heated room and a hot cup of coffee. It was hard to leave the snug oasis of the restaurant, but I held onto the hope that I would return to a heated, lighted home. Just in case, though, I stopped to buy a small stack of wood for ten dollars.

We returned to a cold, dark house. Dismayed but undaunted, I set to the task of starting a fire in the fireplace. It was immediately evident that I had dropped out of girl scouts too early. After having burned every bit of cardboard and paper in the house as kindling, the wood still wouldn't light. The house remained cold.

I didn't know then what "green" wood was. The opportunist selling wood that morning had probably chopped the tree down an hour earlier.

Why, why, why did this have to happen when Eric was out of town?

My girlfriend called. "Derek and I are leaving to go out of town tonight, and we've got power at our apartment. Why don't you bring Jonathan over here to spend the night?"

A couple of hours later, I was making macaroni and cheese in my friend's kitchen. I was lonely for Eric, devoid of electricity, and now I was homesick as well. My only consolation was the homemade whoopie pie my friend had given me as she left. She instinctively knew that chocolate would get me through the night. As thankful as I was for the kindness of my friend, though, I wanted more than anything to be in my own house. I was tired of being a displaced, cold, pregnant woman whose husband was eating fresh seafood while overlooking the Bay in seventy-degree weather.

I couldn't stand it. I called my neighbor.

"Hello, this is Jill Boehme. I was just wondering if the electricity has come back on yet."

Oh, goodness me, it had come on quite a while ago! So glad to know that I had packed up my overnight bags and dragged my toddler and my pregnant belly across town for nothing. No matter. I was going home.

I hadn't realized that I had left every light in the house burning at full tilt. Jonathan and I arrived to a very bright, very warm home. What a beautiful sight! After tucking Jonathan into his own, warm crib, I searched for the whoopie pie. Eating it in my own home would indescribably enhance the experience.

The whoopie pie was missing.

Where could I have stuck it, I wondered in a chocolate panic. In the diaper bag? No, no, I was sure I had had it in my hand as I locked the apartment door. Was it in the car? No, no sign of it. Alas! Back in the warmth of my own house only to be deprived of a homemade whoopie pie!

Why, oh why, oh why did Eric have to be out of town when I needed chocolate?

When Eric arrived home two days later, there were several sections of town that were still without power. The worst part, though, was the severe tree damage. Eric, an avowed tree-lover, was appalled at the devastation. The ice storm had left its mark in such a profound way that, years later, the damage in some areas was still unmistakable.

What about me, though? I had survived the ice storm on my own. I had even survived the loss of the whoopie pie. Why wasn't Eric gushing over my remarkable survival instincts? He had missed the whole thing; I had lived through it. I really expected him to be more impressed.

The whoopie pie resurfaced several months later, between the cushions of my friend's sofa. She never did offer me another one.

I admit, I would not have survived long as a pioneer. I have acquired an intense empathy for women whose husbands travel regularly. And I have learned how to start a fire. I would like to claim that the experience of the ice storm left an indelible mark on my character; that I am a changed woman. In truth, however, it is nothing more than another reason to whine about the difficulties of being left behind by a traveling husband.

In the best of times, my life contains my husband and chocolate. When one of them is temporarily absent, I must rely on the other. If they are both absent – well, there had better not be an ice storm brewing.

Maggie's Mishaps

Some children seem marked for mishap.

One would expect that, having a mixture of boys and girls, one would find a higher percentage of emergencies taking place in the male population of the household. Snakes and snails and puppy dog tails – that sort of thing.

Au contraire. Allow me to introduce you to Maggie, my sweet, slam-bang little girl.

It started at the tender age of fifteen months. Maggie and Jonathan were upstairs playing while Eric and I lounged with my parents, who were visiting for the week. Suddenly, loud wailing erupted from Maggie's bedroom. Beating Eric by mere seconds, I was the first to encounter my screaming toddler.

Blood. I had about ten seconds to steel myself against the sight of the blood streaming from Maggie's mouth before Eric appeared at the bathroom door.

Assuming my most professional demeanor, I announced: "It's a mouth wound. They always look worse than they are."

Moments later, I discovered the slit in Maggie's tongue – like a little mouth, mirthlessly opening and closing as it spewed blood. My calm façade dissolved.

"Oh my gosh, Eric, she bit her tongue! There's a slit in her tongue!"

I am convinced that, if medieval doctors had used the tongue for their bloodletting purposes, they would have been more successful. Of course, a lot more people would have bled to death. I wonder that medical science has not yet discovered that there is an artery that leads directly from the heart to the tongue. At any rate, the amount of blood flowing from a half-inch slice in the tongue of a fifteen-month-old is inconceivable to one who has never had the remarkable experience of attempting to stop it.

Pureed food and daily disinfecting of the wound were all that the doctor ordered. There would be no emergency tongue surgery – there was not even a need for stitches. The gruesome little "mouth" grew smaller and smaller, and finally disappeared.

Maggie's mishaps, however, had just begun.

Having made it to the age of three with her tongue intact, Maggie was naughtily climbing on the deck railing one summer evening, when she suddenly slipped, clonking her top teeth on the rail. Upon examining the teeth, I discovered that the left one had been pushed up out of its normal spot.

Thus began the very slow death of a baby tooth.

The tooth returned to its normal space within a couple of weeks, but it was soon apparent that its color was changing. By the time Maggie was four, the tooth was noticeably gray, and an x-ray revealed that the roots were destroyed. I had the option of getting the tooth pulled, to eliminate the chance of infection.

Anal-retentive people do not get their children's teeth pulled before their time. How could I allow my four-year-old to have a missing top tooth before her six-year-old brother had one? It was out of the question. The tooth would have to die a natural death, which it finally did when Maggie was six. Scores of gray-toothed photographs notwithstanding, I am glad we didn't have the tooth pulled.

The tooth, of course, was a mere trifle compared to what lay ahead.

It was a Sunday evening, and our church group meeting was just underway. One of the group members had taken the children, including four-year-old Maggie, outside to ride their bikes. Not five minutes had passed when Jonathan came bursting through the front door, breathless and urgent.

"Mommy, Maggie is hurt!"

Fearless Maggie had ridden her Big Wheel down the hill in front of our house and had wiped out at the bottom, flying from the three-wheeler and landing chin-first on the parking lot. A call to the doctor's office confirmed what we suspected: Maggie needed stitches.

Leaving the other children in the care of a friend, Eric and I accompanied Maggie on this unforeseen medical adventure. We watched, wide-eyed, as the wound was stitched shut. One stitch. Two. Three.

"Oops, I don't like that one." I winced as the doctor removed the third stitch and administered another, more to her liking.

Then it was all over. Maggie had been brave, and we took her out for an ice cream sundae. I had been brave, too, but I didn't want an ice cream sundae. I was still counting those stitches.

Oh, but there's more.

Two years later, one of our rare, Saturday morning lounges in bed was shattered by a frantic "Mommy!" in the hallway. Jumping up, I met Maggie at the door of our bedroom.

"I hurt myself…"

She held out her hand. It was distorted – disfigured. Her thumb was sticking oddly out of the back of her hand, where it didn't belong. I pulled her into the room and displayed the errant thumb to Eric.

"She jammed her thumb," I announced in the faux-calm voice I had mastered over the years. Never having seen a jammed thumb in my life, I am left wondering from where I had drawn this knowledge.

"Maggie, how did this happen?"

It had happened like any freak accident – freakishly. Maggie had been horseplaying in her room, and had suddenly lost her balance and fallen. In order to catch herself, she had extended her right arm toward the wall – and had caught her thumb on the baseboard.

Scrunch. Hello accordion-thumb.

The thumb had to be pulled back into place, after which it swelled until it was the size and color of an alien plum. X-rays revealed no fractures, and after a week she was as good as new. In the meantime, though, she had to attend her very first ballet class wearing a splint. Not a very good first impression in a class that requires grace and form.

Even now, the injury trend doesn't seem to be ending. Quite recently, Maggie fell off of her bicycle and landed on her face, knocking out a loose tooth, cutting her lip and mangling her

117

chin (not the chin again!). At breakfast the next morning, Eric exclaimed, "Maggie, if you keep this up, you're not going to have any chin left!" She didn't appreciate his humor.

I can chuckle at the recollection of these incidents. There has been no tragedy – no loss of life or limb. For that I am unspeakably grateful. I watch my dichotomous daughter – fluid and graceful in one heartbeat, and lumbering aimlessly in the next – and my prayer is that, as she grows, the grace will overshadow the hapless foolhardiness. In the meantime, I keep an ample supply of Band-Aids and "No-More-Ouchie" spray on hand, and chant my endless reminders: "No running on the aggregate. No wild play in the house. Be ladylike."

When I hear her crying, I brace myself. And when I discover it's only because Jonathan won't let her in the bathroom, I breathe a sigh of relief. Sibling rivalry isn't half as scary as a bleeding toddler or a disfigured thumb.

But that's another story.

Time For Romance

I once knew a mother of three who claimed that she and her husband never went out and left the children with a baby-sitter.

Never.

If my husband had been informed, prior to becoming a father, that he was no longer to have any time alone with his wife, he would have thrown the towel in. He may even have had a vasectomy. In all honesty, I myself would have had severe doubts about motherhood if I thought that it entailed the complete sacrifice of my relationship with Eric.

Three children and nary a night out? Three hundred sixty-five suppers a year, all eaten in the same kitchen with the same loud, crumb-dropping, ketchup-schplopping, milk-spilling gang? Good-bye forever to candlelight dinners at favorite restaurants? No more holding hands over the tiramisu – whispering sweet nothings between sips of Chardonnay – playing footsie under the table?

It makes one wonder if anything romantic had ever occurred *before* the children arrived. For that matter, it makes one wonder how any children arrived in the first place.

Despite the fact that I am completely, desperately, and irrevocably attached to my four children, I crave time alone with my husband. Eric is (I say this without blushing) my Prince Charming. The chaos of home life – and the unavoidable slew of annoying habits that we somehow overlooked during our dating days – needs to be counteracted by time away together. Regularly rediscovering each other on a romantic level keeps the sparks in a marriage that might otherwise fizzle into nothing more than an amiable (or worse!) partnership.

New babies, of course, present a challenge to the romantically inclined; but if the baby is on a regular feeding schedule, it will be much easier to schedule dates with hubby. For instance, if baby nurses at noon, naps from 1:00 to 3:00, then awakes to nurse again, it is very easy to nurse the baby, leave immediately, enjoy a nice lunch with the love of your life, and return in plenty of time for the 3:00 feeding. Evening dates are even easier to schedule, as long as baby has a regular bedtime. When my babies were very small, they nursed each evening around 7:00 and went to bed at 8:00. I would then wake them before I went to bed for a final nursing, after which they slept until morning. Therefore, I was able to leave with Eric after the 7:00 feeding and not worry about returning until the late-night one. Once that late feeding was dropped, scheduling dates became even easier.

As important as it is to meet baby's needs, it is equally important to meet each other's needs. We must nurture the relationship we started out with, or we may lose it.

Dinner or afternoon dates are one thing. Leaving my child overnight, however, was a hurdle I knew I needed to overcome. It was our fifth wedding anniversary, and a night in a hotel room seemed a perfectly romantic way to celebrate (it was also the perfect way to conceive our second child, but that's another story). Jonathan was fourteen months old, and we were going to be parted overnight for the first time. As I wrote out Jonathan's schedule for my sister-in-law, who was going to spend the night with him, I was suddenly struck with the fact that Jonathan was going to eat three meals without me. Three meals! I had never missed watching him eat his morning banana; I had never failed to be the one to spread the peanut butter on his bread at lunchtime. How could I leave him in someone else's care for three entire meals?

My trepidation was short-lived. Eric and I left, had a wonderful time, and returned. Our little boy was happy, unscathed, and emotionally healthy – and, more amazingly, so was I!

Our second overnight date occurred when I was eight months pregnant with Maggie (yes, that would be eight months after our first overnight date). Eric and I had planned on attending a marriage seminar, and married friends of ours were going to spend the night with Jonathan. For months afterward, my friends teased me about the intricate, detailed notes I had left to instruct them in their care of Jonathan. What to feed him – how to discipline him – what he was not allowed to do – when he ate, napped, went to bed – it was a masterpiece of anal retentiveness. I can only hope that I have relaxed somewhat in recent years.

So, I had survived overnight separation, and my marriage had thrived. Was I ready for something bigger?

When Maggie and Jonathan were one and three years old, respectively, I accompanied Eric on a business trip to Orlando. This was a biggy for Mommy Hen: four days and three nights away from her little chickens, who were to be in the loving care of Grandmom and Grandad. As our bus pulled out of the depot and rolled farther and farther away from my waving children, I dissolved in tears. It felt incredibly wrong; I felt the tendons of my soul stretching and ripping with every revolution of those bus wheels. How could I leave my babies behind?

Five minutes later, I was over it. By the time we boarded the plane, I was ecstatic. If it weren't for the fact that I was five months pregnant, I would have felt like a newlywed. I was on my way to Orlando with my wonderful husband – alone! No diapers to change, no mouths to wipe, no bedtimes to adhere to, no strollers to push, no incessant interruptions. This was going to be a real vacation!

And so it was. While Eric spent his days in workshops, I lounged by the pool in the shade of a palm tree, reading Victoria magazine and luxuriating in my aloneness. In the evenings, I delighted in the company of my husband – eating seafood, drinking wine, holding hands. We spent one whole day together at Epcot Center, where, despite the fact that I almost needed a wheelchair at one point from overexertion (it's easy to forget that you're pregnant when you're in love), we enjoyed ourselves as we hadn't in years.

I am ashamed to admit that three years went by before we had another several-day hiatus together. Eric was flying to San Francisco, his favorite city, on business, and he wanted to fly out a few days early – with me. It was hard for me to swallow the number of miles that would be between my three little ones and me. I struggled through a mixture of intense excitement and sheer dread. I bought new shoes, a new dress and a new purse. I worked out a perfect child care schedule that was comprised of four adults and their exact arrival and departure times. (I seemed to derive a measure of comfort from my administrative skills.)

San Francisco was a dream – the perfect getaway. I grinned and squealed through my first trolley ride. I sipped and sauntered my way through the wineries at Napa Valley. I took notes madly on our tour of Victorian houses. In short, I completely lost myself in the city and my husband's company. I did not spend my time worrying about the children's safety or lamenting over the miles between us. When Monday morning dawned and I had to fly home alone, it tore my heart in two. There was no doubt in my mind, or in Eric's: for as devoted as I was to my children, I was completely in love with my husband.

Although three more years (and another pregnancy) passed before Eric and I were able to slip away together again, our most recent romantic adventure was by far the best ever - and worthy of singular attention in a separate essay. I am convinced that our relationship will continue to blossom as we invest uninterrupted time into each other. My relationship with Eric, you see, is the foundation of our family. The enjoyment we derive from being together enhances the enjoyment of our time with the children. If we remain hopelessly, helplessly in love with each other, that will only serve to strengthen the bonds that unite all six of us. I am thrilled – delighted – blessed beyond measure – that I have a husband who adores me, and who craves my company.

What more could I possibly want?

Shopping Cart Escapade

It's not easy being stranded at home all day with four little ones.

Yes, I said "stranded." For many years, when Eric left in the morning, he drove off in our only vehicle. The children and I were housebound until he returned in the evening.

Unless, of course, we walked somewhere.

Taking a walk around the neighborhood, while pleasant, doesn't really give one the sense of actually having gone somewhere, though. Especially when one lives on a circular street, such as ours. Upon returning home, one has literally been walking in circles.

On a particularly warm and cheery Friday morning, it suddenly occurred to me that I wanted to actually *go* somewhere. I wanted to do the grocery shopping. The nearest supermarket was an easy distance on foot, and I thought the children might enjoy the outing. Our double stroller, I thought, would be the ideal instrument for carting home baby and groceries.

Silly me. The double stroller was in the van, which Eric had driven to work.

Undaunted, I strapped Spencer into his umbrella stroller, and off we went. The sun was warmer than I had anticipated, and I had soon peeled off my sweatshirt and tied it around my waist. Since the children were taking turns pushing the stroller, I was free to jauntily swing my arms and enjoy the pleasure of walking in the sunshine with my little ones.

As we approached the parking lot of the store, Maggie asked, "Mommy, how are we going to get the groceries home?"

I smiled. "We'll just push the cart home."

Maggie looked concerned. "Mommy, are we going to ask them for permission to take the cart?"

Well, for goodness sake, I may have been bold enough to borrow the cart, but my pride would never have allowed me to actually ask somebody if I could do it. Naturally, I preferred to be as discreet as possible. I don't think it occurred to me at the time that there is nothing discreet about a woman with four children pushing a shopping cart up the road.

"We don't have to ask," I assured my worried daughter, "because we are going to return the cart."

I was actually able to successfully complete the shopping trip, despite the distraction of having all four of my children along. Free samples of orange slices and cookies helped to sweeten their experience, and the fact that I was getting the shopping done a day early in order to free up my Saturday sweetened mine. I paid for the groceries and triumphantly pushed the cart through the double doors.

Suddenly, I felt self-conscious. It'll look like I'm going to my car, I thought, and no one will notice when I actually leave the premises. I tried to look casual.

Were shopping carts always this loud?

Once out of the parking lot, I felt safer. What a grand adventure, this! It said something for my self-confidence, at any rate. I knew that, five years earlier, I would rather have died than be seen pushing a full shopping cart down the street.

Here I was, the quintessential, suburban bag lady, making a beautiful racket while confidently pushing my groceries home.

"Mommy, I'm tired of pushing Spencer." A predictable complaint from Jonathan.

"Well, I'm sorry, Sweetie. You're going to have to push him because I have to push the cart."

Were shopping carts always this heavy?

I panted. I sweat. I kept pushing that shopping cart – past the cars at the intersection, past the construction workers in our subdivision, past the houses, inhabited and under construction. One of the subcontractors smiled broadly and asked me if I was bringing in the troops.

Circus act, more likely. Make way, ladies and gentleman, make way. Now entering the center ring: the remarkable, the strange, the unpredictable Boehme Family and their amazing shopping cart!

As we passed the only other completed house on our side of the circle, I was immensely grateful that it was a work day, thus ensuring that Mindy and her husband weren't home. I was already a bit of an anomaly to Mindy: a stay-at-home, homeschooling mother of four with no car and, I'm sure she assumed, no life. I had no desire to confirm her suspicions of my eccentricity by parading by with my children and a shopping cart.

At last, we made it. Unseen by any familiar eyes. Unbeknownst to my husband, who would have handcuffed me to the kitchen table before allowing me to make such a spectacle of myself. The shopping cart was safely in the garage, and my overheated children were gratefully guzzling cold water.

Live and let live! Seize the day! Walk to the beat of a different drummer! I had triumphed.

The next day I stood out front, chatting pleasantly with Mindy, who, in the middle of our light conversation, dropped a bombshell.

"Was that you I saw yesterday pushing a shopping cart?"

How could she have seen me? No one was supposed to see me.

"You saw me?"

Why yes, she explained, she was working from home yesterday, when suddenly she had looked out the window and had seen a woman pushing a shopping cart by her house, with four children in tow.

"I thought," said Mindy, "that it looked like you, and I figured you must have been on an outing with the kids."

How quaint! Mindy – attractive, professional, I've-got-it-all-together Mindy – was amused during her at-home workday by the sudden appearance of her wacky neighbor pushing a shopping cart down the road.

Truly, I was horrified, but I seized the opportunity to laugh at myself while attempting to explain to Mindy the reasons for my shopping cart excursion. My storytelling soon had her belly laughing, though I couldn't help but wonder if she was secretly concerned about my sanity. I am sure that Mindy came away from that conversation very thankful that her life was nothing at all like mine.

I exist for the amusement of my neighbors.

And what, you may ask, became of the shopping cart? It sat innocently in our garage for two weeks until I finally persuaded Eric that, since I had gone through the trouble of bringing home the groceries in it, he could certainly be kind enough to return the cart for me. Of course, he was much more discreet than I had been. He loaded the cart into the back of the van and drove it back to the store. I'm sure the removal of a cart from the back of a van was an equally strange exhibit, though of course there were no neighbors lurking about while Eric accomplished his task.

No, indeed. These things only happen to me.

Supermom

Faster than a vomiting child. Stronger than a two-week pile of dirty diapers. Able to clear a clogged toilet in a single plunge. It's a bird. It's a plane. It's...

What exactly is it, anyway?

I am suspicious that underneath the sweating, disheveled, slobbered-on, plunger-wielding creature is a woman whom I used to know. She is vaguely familiar. Those eyes, if they weren't so tired, would have a familiar sparkle. And those fingers – haven't I seen them playing Mozart sonatas? The feet are familiar, too – there aren't too many women who wear a size five. If I could just get a better look at her....

Why, it's me!

This is not a pretty sight. I demand to see my job description.

What? I entered into this highest of callings without a written and detailed job description? I've been duped! But wait – it is a mere trifle for me to produce a list of my daily tasks.

NURTURER: Duties to include all of the following: Rocking crying babies, cuddling sleepy children, bathing dirty bodies, wiping stinky bottoms, brushing tangled hair, kissing sticky cheeks, holding tiny hands, singing endless songs, and figuring out how to share one tired lap with four needy children.

ENCOURAGER: Duties to include all of the following: Determining the individual giftings of each child and providing opportunities for growth in these areas; never accepting "I can't" as a legitimate answer; reminding each child daily why he is so special; displaying artwork and other tangible accomplishments; paying close attention every time a child explains an idea, shares a creation, or tells a story; and being the tireless family cheerleader when you have absolutely no energy left.

HOUSECLEANER: Duties to include all of the following: Cleaning and maintenance of the kitchen, living room, dining room, parlor, family room, hallway, bathrooms (three) and bedrooms (five), including weekly dusting, sweeping, wiping, scrubbing, spraying, vacuuming, mopping, straightening, disinfecting, deodorizing, or whatever else needs to be done, despite the fact that your children are screaming and you couldn't care less if your house burns down, much less whether or not it is presentable when your husband comes home.

NURSE: Duties to include all of the following: Tending to the medical needs of the children at all times, including wiping boogies, removing tics, washing out scrapes and cuts, applying Band-Aids, removing bloodstains from shirts, cleaning up vomit, administering medicine, taking temperatures, adjusting bed pillows, consulting with the pediatrician, providing transportation to and from all medical facilities, teaching proper bottom-wiping etiquette to little girls (front to back), applying calamine lotion to bug bites and poison, spraying Lysol on all easily-contaminated surfaces, picking up prescriptions at the pharmacy, trimming fingernails, discerning between real emergencies and dramatic performances, rubbing the growing-pains out of legs at midnight, and frantically reminding your daughters to never, never touch a public toilet as long as they live.

PROBLEM-SOLVER: Duties to include all of the following: Finding a lost sneaker when everyone else is in the van waiting to leave for an appointment; dividing the number of jellybeans by four and eating any remainder yourself; figuring out whose turn it is to sit in the front of the tub; determining which child is telling the truth in the midst of a dispute; getting the entire family ready for church in less than thirty minutes; coming up with a nutritious dinner at the end of the week when there is nothing but saltines, tuna, and a can of tomato paste in the pantry; getting the children to brush their teeth when the bubble-gum flavored toothpaste is gone; having an intelligible phone conversation while the children are eating lunch at the top of their lungs; and getting your children's names straight when you call them.

ADMINISTRATIVE SECRETARY: Duties to include all of the following: Making and keeping all appointments for doctor and dentist visits, haircuts, party invitations, and photograph sittings; presenting three meals a day at consistent intervals; employing the use of a timer to ensure that certain boys don't spend an hour and ten minutes in the bathtub and still say, "but I haven't washed yet;" overseeing the timely completion of piano practice – particularly when it is under duress; delegating household chores and refraining from nagging about their completion; preparing a schedule for exactly whose turn it is on the computer, and how long that turn will last; keeping track of library books and their due dates – and being determined to finally return the two that you have had for three years from a library in the county in which you no longer live; making sure that no hermit crab is at risk of starvation; carefully counting the sheets of paper each child uses for artistic pursuits, so that the entire ream isn't used up in four days; endeavoring to schedule some adult socializing even if you've forgotten how to do so; and occasionally informing your husband what is going on so that he can be somewhat involved in the mechanics of life as you know it.

TECHICIAN/REPAIRMAN: Duties to include all of the following: On-demand repairing of children's necklaces, Barbie legs, broken plastic horses, VCR's, die-cast cars, computer programs, computer keyboards, televisions, lamps, torn clothing, bicycles, hairbrushes, doorknobs, cassette tapes, speakers, flip flops, toy watches, torn books, ballet shoes, bike helmets, tape recorders, dolly heads, headbands, window shades, iron beds, vacuum cleaners, hair dryers, shower curtains, stuffed animals, pencils, remote controls, wooden chairs, paintbrushes, ceiling fans and closet doors.

In addition to the above-mentioned, duties will also include the following: REFEREE, COOK, TEACHER, IN-HOUSE 911 OPERATOR, PLUMBER, INTERIOR DECORATOR, LAUNDRESS, DRILL SARGEANT, TRANSLATOR, MEAL PLANNER, HOSTESS and WIFE.

"WIFE," by the way, has its own, separate job description.

Nowhere in my list of duties do I find the following: "Soaking in a bubbling hot tub for one hour each night;" "Enjoying a glass of Chardonnay while the children prepare dinner;" or "Spending two weeks with hubby at the seashore, luxuriating in having to do absolutely nothing." I think I would settle for, "Eating one Godiva truffle while sitting quietly on the bottom step." Indeed, my life is not one of glamour or leisure! Somewhere in the sea of filtered-lens photographs of beautiful women in flowing, white gowns holding perfect babies in flowing, white gowns, the true picture has been lost. A few snapshots of my daily life will serve to enlighten the most casual observer.

Yes, I do spend a lot of time unclogging toilets. Yes, I am quite proud of the muscles in my upper arms, developed from child-lifting instead of weight-lifting. And yes, I am perfectly happy doing what I do. Don't expect me to be wearing lipstick when I answer the door; for that matter, don't even expect me to answer the door (I may not hear the doorbell over the din). Don't ask my opinion on which brand of pantyhose lasts the longest, or which shampoo works best for dry hair (they're all the same to me). If you have a question on diaper brands or toilet bowl cleaner, though, I'm all ears. I have attained expertise in scores of areas in which I never actively pursued knowledge. Men may not gaze in rapt admiration as I glide (or stumble) through a doorway, but my children think I'm wonderful.

Motherhood has a glamour all its own. I wouldn't trade it for anything.

Coloring My Hair

The time had come.

My list of "I wish I could's" had been growing exponentially: "I wish I could have a full-body massage. I wish I could drive a Miata. I wish I could get all of my facial hair removed. I wish I could spend $5,000 on a new wardrobe." On and on the list trailed - a mental escape from my not-too-glamorous existence. If only...if only...if only. There's something about wearing frumpy clothes and getting spit up on that affects self-esteem in a way that only mothers can understand. There were days on which I felt almost desperate.

I missed my chance for the massage. My mother, dear soul that she is, sent me $50 for my thirty-second birthday so that I could go get a massage. The money sat in my drawer for months. Somehow, I simply couldn't get myself to make that appointment. Stripping down and letting a stranger massage me was more than my level of self-confidence could bear. Fantasizing about a massage was much easier than actually receiving one. So I spent the fifty dollars on clothes.

Of course, the "I wish" that was dearest to my heart was, "I wish I could go blonde." Mind you, I had been born blonde - not a true "tow head," but with tresses that were definitely of the golden variety. As a teenager I could often be spied pouring lemon juice on my hair and lying in the sun, hoping to wake up platinum. All I ever got was a bad sunburn - and sticky hair. Like most blondes, my hair continued to darken as I grew older. I never obsessed about it, but I wasn't too happy with it, either. Once I asked a hairdresser, "What color would you call my hair?" He squinted at me, thought for a moment, and then replied, "Caramel."

Caramel? I did not want "caramel" hair. Caramel is for pouring on ice cream and wrapping around apples. He had no business telling me that I had "caramel" hair.

Things definitely got worse after the birth of my firstborn. Through some mysterious, hormonal function that my doctor neglected to inform me about, my hair darkened beyond "caramel." Not only was I fast losing my "blonde" status (however tenuous that hold may have been), but my first gray hairs were far too visible against so dark a background.

Over the next several years, I watched in helpless agony as my hair continued to darken after each pregnancy. There are those, I am sure, who still would have qualified me as a "dark blonde," but to someone who longed for pale tresses, this was a nightmare.

You may be thinking, "Why in the world didn't you color your hair?"

That's a good question. And I have a good answer, too. You see, I thought that only insecure women colored their hair - that somehow, if I colored my hair, I would be displaying some kind of insecurity in my identity. Why, I needed to rise above this and prove to myself that I was more than the sum of my parts – including my hair color!

I'm serious. I wouldn't color my hair for that reason.

Penny, my hairdresser, was a saint. She listened patiently as I lamented about my hair color. She knew that I wanted to be blonde, but I just didn't have it in me to take the leap.

"You really should get it highlighted," she recommended. "Highlighting fades gradually, so you don't end up with dark roots. I think you'll really like it."

I wasn't so sure. What if my hair ended up looking "striped" like so many other women I'd seen? Of course, I couldn't say *that* to Penny, who sported a headful of highlighted hair.

So, I settled for a new hairstyle. Several months later, I opted for a different hairstyle. And after that, a third. As time passed and I finally found a style that suited me, my courage began to swell. Maybe highlighting *wouldn't* be such a bad idea. Maybe it was time - finally, finally time - for a change. I had told myself for years that if I didn't color my hair before I turned forty, I would never color it at all. I was still several years away from my self-imposed time limit when I suddenly found that I had it in me after all.

The main ingredient in my change of heart, though, was my husband. Eric's encouragement was the little push I needed to make the appointment. There were times when he would almost drool as he'd murmur, "I want you to go blonde." And this from a man who several years earlier had scoffed at the idea! Truly, I knew he'd love me no matter what color my hair was. But there was something about that drool...

At any rate, I made the appointment. I'm not sure if Penny was proud of me or simply relieved that I'd gotten over my neurosis. She had been my hairdresser for nine years, and there was no one I would have trusted more with what for me was a huge affair. In the six weeks that lay between the blonde highlights and me, I lost ten pounds and bought several new outfits for our upcoming vacation. The new hair color would be the icing on the cake.

A week before the appointment, Eric took the boys for haircuts. "Well," he said as Penny snipped away, "Next Saturday's the big day!"

"Oh, are you leaving for vacation?" Snip. Snip.

"No, Jill is getting her hair colored," Eric reminded her.

"Oh! Well, yeah, I guess that *is* a big day!" Clearly it wasn't a big day for Penny.

And, so, one week later, there I sat. Penny, having seen me through many a hair crisis, looked a bit worried. "Penny, I'm not uptight," I assured her. "I'm really okay with this!"

And I was! Somehow I had finally gotten to the point at which I was thinking, "Hey! It's only hair." Getting a tattoo had to be scarier than this.

Penny visibly relaxed once she realized I wasn't nervous.

"Do you want to see some samples of blonde, or do you want me to pick it?"

"You pick it." The last thing I needed to be faced with was a choice. Anyway, I trusted Penny implicitly.

Ninety minutes later, my hair was streaked with blonde the likes of which it had never seen. Jumping out of an airplane could not possibly have been as exhilarating as this very personal moment. Why in the world hadn't I done this years ago?

The children were lavish with their praise: "Mommy, I LOVE it! You look GORGEOUS!" Throughout the day, Jonathan - my little nine-year-old who is obsessed with bugs and wildflowers and bike riding - continued to compliment my hair. He is going to make someone an outstanding husband!

As for Eric - he hasn't stopped grinning at me. "Do you feel sexy?" he'll say with a glance at my blonde locks. I remind him that it isn't the hair that makes me feel sexy - it's his admiration.

My Lima Beans Are Allergic To My Spoon

It is beyond thrilling to know that he is pleased with what he sees.

I'm sure there are women out there who *do* color their hair because they are insecure. But I now believe that there are women - like me - who color their hair because they are *secure* enough to do so! If I had been paralyzed by worrying if I'd hate it, wondering what people would think, or simply by being afraid of change, I would have missed out on the wonderful boost to my self-image. I feel like I haven't lost the enjoyment of simply being a woman, after all. I may even tackle new make-up or high heels next - or maybe I'll get that massage, after all.

Spending my days in old shorts and stained shirts doesn't steal my womanhood - as long as I don't let it. Mothering my children, to me, is the epitome of femininity; the apex of my calling as a woman. But the feisty, quick-witted woman with whom my husband fell in love is alive and well - and now she's blonde, too!

Discipline and Character

On Rude Kids and Mom's Bathroom Habits

I couldn't help overhearing the animated conversation between two mothers at swimming lessons today.

"When do you take a shower?" the first one asked.

The second mother proceeded to explain how she had a clear, glass shower, so that she could easily see what was going on. I couldn't help wondering what could possibly be "going on" in the bathroom while she was bathing herself. She went on to say that she always brought one child in the bathroom with her and let him have his bath while she showered. Her morning shower plan worked, she claimed, and besides, she didn't like taking showers at night.

"Oh, neither do I!" said the first. She then explained how she had to hurry through her shower in the morning, hoping that her children would stay occupied during the process. She bemoaned the fact that there was no television upstairs, which deprived her of an instant babysitter.

"Of course, Brandon always ends up banging and rattling at the door the whole time," she finished despairingly. "I just can't get the time to myself!"

Am I missing something here?

I will be the first one to admit that I am not the Perfect Mother. This little dilemma, however, seems terribly simple to solve: GET UP BEFORE THE CHILDREN DO.

Now, it may well be that these poor, privacy-deprived mothers had housefuls of early risers with whom they could not possibly compete. I offer yet another surprisingly simple answer: TRAIN YOUR CHILDREN TO ALLOW YOU PRIVACY.

What? Train my child to do what?

It never ceases to amaze me when parents do not take authority over their children's behavior, only to lament loudly about it to whomever will listen. "He always interrupts me when I'm on the phone." "I can't get him to stop throwing food at the table." "Every time I sit down to read a magazine, she climbs on my lap and wants to play."

Excuse me, but who's in charge here? If a child is calling all the shots, then something isn't quite right. I do get up before everyone else in the morning, and I take my shower in peace. There are times, however, when my son is up before I'm in the shower. He would never dream of banging on the bathroom door or bothering me in any other way. Why? Because my husband and I have trained him, over the course of several years, that Mommy always needs privacy when she's in the bathroom. It's as simple as that. He knows to wait for me, and if I am taking too long to emerge from the bathroom after the water has stopped running, he will knock politely on the door. He knows that I might not be dressed, and he has been trained to respect the privacy of others.

If Mom needs thirty minutes to get rid of a headache or ten minutes for a quick phone call, it is not unrealistic to expect the children to respect her space. Part of training children to obey is teaching them that Mom (Dad, too) needs some time alone, without interruption. Children will exhibit whatever behavior we consistently allow them to get away with. If we grit our teeth through phone interruptions, barging into bathrooms, and constant door banging while we're taking a ten-minute rest, we are doing our children and ourselves a disservice.

I spend a lot of time with my children, seven days a week. If I allow them to sabotage the times that I DO set aside to accomplish something on my own (or to simply lie down in a quiet room!), I will burn out more quickly, and I will inadvertently teach them that it is okay to demand people's attention at any time, without respect for the individual's time or personal needs.

The last thing society needs is more self-absorbed people!

Teach your children to knock before entering a room. Teach them that it is not all right to bang on a door for twenty minutes. Dole out immediate consequences when they interrupt a phone call (I once read the words of a mother who claimed that she told her children that they were only allowed to interrupt her if someone was bleeding from the head). Take the extra effort to train them. If you don't, then please don't whine about their behavior. As parents, we all daily reap what we have sown.

Fussy Eaters

Recently, while standing in the checkout line in a grocery store, I overheard a man's conversation with another customer. The man's shopping cart was loaded down with jars of baby food – enough to feed an entire platoon of ten-month-olds.

"He won't eat anything except baby food," the domesticated dad was saying. "He doesn't eat anything that's solid. Nothing! Even if we give him baby food with chunks in it, he sucks the liquid off and spits the chunks out."

I couldn't help wondering if the child would still be eating pureed food on his fourth birthday.

All children inevitably flex their opinion muscles when it comes to food. Those of us who are more high-strung tend to worry constantly that our child is not getting adequate nutrition. "When he had his first carrots, he loved them; now all he wants is applesauce!" "I try to feed her the cereal, but she just screams until I offer her my breast." "How can my toddler survive on Cheerios and Velveeta?"

During my firstborn's babyhood, I had a fairly easy time. Jonathan was unlikely to reject anything that was offered to him. He opened his little mouth equally wide for jarred carrots, green beans, or pears. When he graduated to table food, he was well known for enjoying broccoli, raw cucumbers, and fresh pineapple. Of course, Jonathan didn't have any "sweets" until he turned two, which made it easier to introduce healthier, less sweet foods. To him, a slice of cantaloupe was dessert from heaven. The only thing Jonathan never really liked was potatoes. I could live with that!

Interestingly, as Jonathan grew out of his preschool years, he became more and more particular about food. Broccoli was no longer the choice du jour. Sandwiches were rejected if they contained even a trace of mayonnaise. By the time he turned eight, Jonathan was informing me that he only liked Peter Pan peanut butter; that frozen vegetables didn't taste good; and that milk was gross. Potatoes remained on the hit list, too, unless they were served in the form of McDonald's french fries. Funny, though, how Jonathan hadn't marked anything off of his refined sugar list. Brownies, ice cream, and homemade apple cobbler remained equally appealing.

Do I smell a direct correlation between the amount of sugar in a child's diet and the amount of healthy foods he will eat?

Regardless of my desire to feed my children a healthy diet, I have an aversion to the "clean plate club." I can't imagine how forcing a child to gag down a mouthful of much-hated spinach or squash will produce a healthy eater in future years.

I have a clear memory of an appalling scenario in the school cafeteria. I was in first grade, and it was Friday, the only day on which I ate lunch at school. Canned lima beans had been the vegetable of the day, and evidently most of the children had overlooked them. As I stood in line to empty my garbage into the can, I noticed one of the teachers standing beside it, fork in hand. As each child approached the garbage can, the teacher filled the fork with lima beans from the child's tray and scooped them into his mouth. I watched in horror as each child in the line was subjected to a forced lima bean feeding.

Fortunately, I had brought my lunch from home, and I didn't have to swallow any slimy lima beans. I imagine that the unlucky children who met up with the fork-wielding lima bean maniac grew up loathing the vegetable. Cruel, inhuman torture – trapped in a line that led to a mouthful of cold lima beans!

Come to think of it, I hate lima beans.

My own children have come up with clever ways of avoiding distasteful foods: "These vegetables got too cold and now I can't eat them." "This meat is too hard to chew." "I'm not hungry anymore." I have witnessed children wiping pizza sauce off of a slice of pizza with a napkin, sorting mixed vegetables according to which were palatable, and, yes, hiding carrots underneath a Tupperware plate (and this by a twenty-two-month old!). It is amazing to note, of course, that a child who is "too full" to finish his mashed potatoes is almost never "too full" to have some dessert. I have often wondered if my children were born with second stomachs that accommodate only sweets.

Dessert is by no means a nightly occurrence at our house. When I do offer it, though, it is with the following condition: "You will finish your dinner." This strategy is not to be confused with the "clean plate club." If there's something on the dinner plate that one of my children dislikes, I expect him to only eat a reasonable amount of it if he wants dessert. He is free to choose not to eat it, in lieu of dessert. I never force my children to eat anything.

I have tried the "there are little children in the world who die because they have no food" speech, but, while this does evoke some level of concern, it has had no long-term effect on my children's eating habits. I may be good at postulating and sermonizing, but these are skills that are better left out of the parenting arena. Children know only what they live. If they are presented with a casserole that turns their stomachs, it makes no difference to them that a child in India would gladly eat it without complaining (although, in the case of some of the casseroles I've come up with, that might be a bit presumptuous).

The bottom line is, if their eating habits are a bit quirky from time to time, our children are not going to cease to thrive. As long as we are neither force-feeding our children nor relinquishing control to their caprices, mealtimes will be largely stress-free and will result in well-fed youngsters. Limiting junk food goes without saying, but the surprise of a treat once in a while goes a long way in maintaining a positive attitude about food.

As for me, I would gladly eat an entire can of lima beans for a bowl of Ben and Jerry's Phish Food ice cream – wouldn't you?

"No" Means "No"

Is it me, or is there an inherent problem with the word "no" that repeatedly causes children to question its meaning?

If I say, "No, not before supper" in response to a request for a piece of candy, why am I met with an immediate dissertation on the sundry reasons why candy at this point in time will not adversely affect the dinner hour?

Dissertations do not change my mind. "NO" means "NO."

If I respond, "No, not right now" to a plea for a video, why does a chorus of mournful whines ("Pleeeeeeeeeease, Mommy....") assault my ears before I draw my next breath, as if my immovable heart will suddenly melt and bend to the whim of my eager and insistent daughter?

Theatrical whining does not change my mind. "NO" means "NO."

And if I state, "No, you need to finish your lunch first" when begged for a reprieve from the table in order to join Daddy outside in the garden, why am I suddenly besieged with negotiation the likes of which could be found in the board rooms of any Fortune 500 company?

Negotiation does not change my mind. "NO" means "NO."

Honestly, I am not one of those wimpy mothers who gives in at the slightest hint of puppy-dog-eyes and pouty lips. In looking carefully at my use of the word "no" over the years, I can truthfully say that my "no" has always been firm. It is a rare moment in which you will see me waiver and then say, "Well...all right."

That may be all it takes. One moment of weakness - one victory for the whining youngster - and immeasurable ground is lost. If Mommy gave in *just that one time*, then she's bound to do it again. Even if that "just once" happened months ago, its effect surely hasn't been lost on those who benefited from it.

There is another strange phenomenon concerning the word "no," however, that I simply cannot account for. It would seem that "no" to a particular request by one sibling does not preclude the identical request from being made by the next:

"Mommy," Maggie says, "May I please have some dessert?"

"No," I respond. "We are not having dessert today."

"Mommy," Rachel pipes up. "May I please have some dessert?"

"Rachel, I just told Maggie that we are not having any dessert today."

Slight pause. Devilish grin from my eldest son.

"Mommy," Jonathan says, his eyes twinkling. "May I please have some dessert?"

I ignore him.

Then, of course, the professional begging kicks in from the female sector:

"Mommy, pleeeeeeease may we have some dessert? How about some graham crackers? Oooooooh, I just want some dessert, Mommy, pleeeeeeeease!"

Do I break down and serve up the ice cream and cookies at this point? Do I smile like Donna Reed and say, in an oozy voice, "Well, darlings, you've been such GOOD little children, I think I WILL give you some dessert!"

NO!

Fact is, I almost never have any dessert in the house, and they know it. Yet somehow this act is played out time and again, in the hopes that maybe there has been a reality shift and the pantry now contains nothing but cupcakes and candy bars.

Mind you, there are times at which negotiation is appropriate. I am sometimes too quick to say "no" to very reasonable requests, and it often happens out of my own impatience and unwillingness to deal with inconvenience:

"Mommy, may I ride my bike?"

"No, it's bath time soon."

"Mommy, what time is it?"

"It's 7:15."

"Well, how about if I ride my bike until 8:00, and then take my bath?"

When presented with such clear logic from a nine-year-old, how could I possibly maintain my original position? In this case, it makes more sense to say, "You're right, Jonathan, that's a good plan. But you need to come in right at 8:00."

Does this make me a pushover? I don't think so. There is a big difference between breaking down because somebody's whining at you, and reconsidering because somebody's made a good point.

Still, the word "no" remains problematic. And I am beginning to suspect that it may have something to do with Daddy.

Allow me to elaborate. On Friday night, Jonathan forgets to get a drink before his 9:00 bedtime. "Mommy," he says, "may I go downstairs and get some water? I forgot to get some and it's a little after nine and I'm really thirsty." My response? "No, you know you are not allowed to go downstairs after 9:00. You may get a drink in the bathroom." Since Jonathan would rather die of thirst than drink tepid tap water, he grumbles off to bed.

On Saturday night we have company. Jonathan comes to the door of the family room and says, "It's a few minutes after nine, but may I go downstairs and get a drink?" Mommy opens her mouth to speak, but before she gets a word out, Daddy says, "Yes, Jonathan, you may." Mommy waits until Jonathan has left the room, and then she gives Daddy a hard slap on the leg. The guests withhold comment.

It is not easy to be consistent - but oh, how we must strive for it! If we send our children confusing, conflicting signals, there will not be solid boundaries in place. "No" will become as meaningless as "maybe" or "ask me later."

I don't like to hear the word "no," either - especially if I've just asked my husband to buy me some chocolate. But "no" is a word we must learn to live with graciously, both in the doling-out and the receiving. Saying "no" can win an argument, strengthen a relationship, protect a child, or save a life. I have found, too, that saying "no" gently is far more effective than barking it out like a drill sergeant. The word "no" doesn't make Mommy the enemy - unless she *acts* that way.

My two-year-old has the sweetest response of all. When I tell him "no," he says, "Okay!" in as cheerful a voice as he can muster - and then he starts to cry. Somehow he, out of all my children, understands that my "no" means "no," and he lets me know that he's going to comply *before* he shows his distress. Oh, the things we can learn from a toddler!

"No." I'm going to keep saying it. I have faith that some day my children will thank me.

Six Cheeseburgers and a Tampon

Yes, it happened to me.

There we were, sitting in our slimy, little booth at McDonald's, waiting for Daddy to bring us our burgers. I was busy disinfecting the high chair for my toddler (have you ever noticed how disgusting those things are?), and, unbeknownst to me, my four-and-a-half-year-old daughter was rummaging through my purse.

Suddenly, in what seemed like a very loud voice, she announced,

"Mommy, I found a tampon!"

My heart skipped a beat as I watched her waving the prized object in the air like some sort of nautical flag. Quickly, I arrested her little hand, grabbed the tampon and flipped it back into my purse.

"Honey, please leave that in there."

Out it came again, in a flash. "Mommy, I know what this is for!" Once again the tampon was proudly displayed for the viewing pleasure of the entire restaurant. She may as well have been flashing a detailed chart of my menstrual cycle.

I found myself in the midst of a dilemma. I am raising my children – male and female – to be free of shame. I want them to feel good about their bodies and the natural functions that go along with them (well, all right, they don't necessarily need to feel good about farting, but I do stress the fact that relieving gas is a natural bodily function, albeit a somewhat offensive one). How was I to get that tampon out of public view without sending the signal that I was somehow ashamed of it?

Yes, I know, there is a time and place to discuss things. Clearly McDonald's was not the place, and public dinner hour was not the time. Teaching our children about their bodies is something that, in my opinion, should be an ongoing, natural dialogue that flows out of daily life. Where do babies come from...why does food go in as food and come out as poopy...and, yes, what are tampons for; these are all valid topics of conversation that definitely count as "health class" in a homeschooling environment. Coupled with the information, of course, is the necessity of teaching tact: "By the way, we do not discuss Mommy's leaking breast milk in Sunday School."

The amount of information we dole out should be in proportion to the child's age and maturity level. A five-year-old who asks, "Where did I come from?" does not need a detailed lesson on human sexuality and the reproductive cycle. We do not need to feed children more than they are asking for; similarly, we should not insult their intelligence by stating, "Well, that's something you aren't ready to understand." Both of my daughters know that Mommy gets her "period" each month because no baby is growing inside her, and there is no need for a nice, soft "home" for one. Beautifully simplified, this information has given them an age-appropriate understanding of what Mommy's tampons are for, and prepares them for the awakening of their own female sexuality. The more natural I am about my body, the less my daughters will fear the changes in their own.

Of course, that does not mean that I enjoy seeing my tampons on display at McDonald's. Then again, there have been worse moments.....

I had sent my six-year-old in to make Mommy and Daddy's bed (for some reason, this is usually perceived as some sort of special treat). I was busy sorting laundry in the hallway, when she emerged from my bedroom, holding something in her hand.

"Mommy, what's this?" My blood froze in my veins.

It was a condom.

Not in a wrapper, and (thankfully!) not used. But there it was, in her little hand. She began to giggle. I began to blush.

"This looks really funny, Mommy. What is it?"

I stammered. I stumbled. I said, "Um...oh..hmmm...it looks like a balloon, doesn't it?"

I grabbed it and threw it away, and, trying to appear casual, I returned to my laundry.

Well, at least I didn't lie. They do look a little bit like balloons. Don't they?

I think there may be a few things I'm not quite ready for. Things that make tampon broadcasts in McDonald's look like a piece of cake.

This Is For Grandmom

Children can be painfully tactless.

It is an unfortunate truth that my husband and I do not share a close relationship with his parents. Nevertheless, we do our best to shelter our children from the true state of affairs. Children love freely and innocently, and Eric and I know that this unconditional love might yet serve as a healing balm for our children's paternal grandparents.

Our relationship with my own parents is, fortunately, warm and loving. I am thankful for the role that they play in our lives, and the children adore them.

Since my parents and in-laws live only two and a half hours from each other, we often spend a couple of days with the latter in the midst of an extended stay with the former. It was during one of these visits that my mother-in-law provided the children with some Play-Doh and cookie cutters to keep them busy. Needless to say, they were delighted, and spent the greater part of the afternoon indulging in artistic creation.

It was shortly before our departure that my mother-in-law proudly displayed a Play-Doh Christmas tree. "Jonathan said he made this for me," she announced with uncharacteristic warmth. "I'm going to save this forever." Happy that my children had once again blessed their grandparents, I began to gather up all of our belongings for the ride back to my parents' home. Good-byes were said as we herded the children into the van. Then I noticed Jonathan carrying the sainted Play-Doh tree.

"Jonathan, didn't you give that to Grandma?" I asked.

"No, Mommy, she misunderstood me. I made this for Grandmom."

My stomach dropped. "You...you didn't tell her that, did you?"

He had. In Jonathan's six-year-old mind, it had been a simple miscommunication. I knew, however, with sickening certainty, that forfeiting a beloved gift had dealt a murderous blow to my mother-in-law. "I'm going to save this forever," she had said.

"I'm going to save this forever." I kept hearing it over and over. I knew something had to be done.

It was shortly after our arrival at my parents' home that Jonathan presented my mother with the Play-Doh Christmas tree. She smiled and gushed and thanked him, and he was glad that the treasure was in the hands of its rightful owner.

I had no peace of mind.

Eric had brought his father's laptop along to my parents' house, in order to install an Internet service provider. In a day or two, his parents would be swinging by to pick up the computer and receive a quick lesson from their son on how to connect to the Internet. In the midst of grumbling about the inconvenience of the proposed visit, it suddenly occurred to me that this would provide the opportunity to make things right.

"Jonathan, I need to talk with you about something."

Gently, I explained to Jonathan that, when he had made the Christmas tree, Grandma had thought it was for her. When he took it away and told her that it was actually for Grandmom, it hurt her feelings. Did he understand why that had hurt her feelings?

Jonathan's tender heart surfaced at once and he was immediately concerned for Grandma's feelings. I then explained that, even though he had originally meant to give the tree to Grandmom, Grandma would be blessed if he were to return the gift to her.

Unhesitatingly, he agreed.

Having already explained the situation to my very down-to-earth mother, I knew she wouldn't have a problem with his asking her to return the Christmas tree so that he could give it to Grandma.

The meeting between families was awkward. My parents had not seen my in-laws for years, and, while there was graciousness all around, I for one would have liked to crawl through the cracks in the hardwood floor. Still, I was in charge of a little boy with a mission, and so, at the appropriate moment, I quietly told Jonathan to fetch the Christmas tree.

He approached his grandmother and placed the tree in her hands. "I want you to have this," he said.

For a moment, she was silent – flabbergasted. Then, her eyes suddenly moist and sparkling, she smiled and thanked Jonathan profusely. I knew that the meaning of the gift was more than she could possibly express – perhaps even more than she herself knew. She cradled the gift as if it were an irreplaceable treasure. I caught Jonathan's eye and smiled my approval.

Jonathan, my passionate, temperamental son, had risen to the occasion and returned a gift to one for whom it had not been intended. I was remarkably proud of him. I saw in him seeds of compassion and understanding well beyond his years. This lesson in respecting the feelings of others had done more to shape his character than I could have accomplished in a year of sermons.

Well done, little guy. I hope that Mommy, too, will learn to so graciously right her own mistakes.

Sexual Purity

I squinted at the crumpled wrapper in the waste can, trying to make out the unusual word printed on it. After sounding it out silently a time or two, I headed for the kitchen.

"Mom, what's a 'prophylactic?'"

She didn't miss a beat. "Oh, that's medicine for your dad's penis."

Not wanting to probe into what could possibly be wrong with my father's genitals, I accepted the answer at face value. Years later, upon remembering the incident, I could only marvel at my mother's quick, if not slightly odd, response.

It is an inevitable passage for every child, that journey from innocence to sexuality. In our sexually saturated culture, it becomes an ever-increasing challenge to keep our children from being prematurely exposed to sex. In the guidebook to Gary and Marie Ezzo's tape series "Reflections of Moral Innocence," the authors write, "We believe it is right to let children be innocent as long as they can, and we believe it is wrong to rush children into adulthood. All of us get only one childhood. What are you doing to protect it for your children? There is no faster way to rob a child of the innocence of childhood than with inappropriate sex education." [2]

Sexually inappropriate material may be so subtle that many parents look past it without a flinch. The scantily clad heroines in today's animated films and television cartoons are a far cry from the chaste Cinderella of yesteryear. Sexual imagery and innuendo is rife in every branch of media. More and more children's clothing styles – particularly for girls – have become scaled-down versions of their sexy, bare-midriff, junior-sized counterparts. Should I choose to protect my children from these offenders, I find that I have more warfare ahead as I steer them past countless posters of nearly naked women in the store windows of our local malls.

It seems that we, as a culture, have lost our sense of modesty, which is the necessary precursor to sexual purity. Teaching our children to love and respect their bodies enough to remain modest, and training them to uphold the privacy of others, will go a long way in the battle to keep our children sexually healthy. Simple gestures, such as knocking on bathroom and bedroom doors before entering, reap life-long habits of respect and decency. Along with this, we should be fostering in our children a healthy love for their own physiology. A child who is taught that there is something inherently shameful about his "private parts" will grow into a sexually unhealthy adult. Modesty, respect, and self-love play equal roles in the positive sexual maturation of our children.

Every child will come to the point at which he is emotionally and intellectually mature enough to understand the facts of life. No responsible parent wants his child to receive this information from an outside source, and certainly not prematurely! My own "revelation" occurred, at the hands of some "informed" friends from school, when I was ten. While sitting at the dinner table that night, I announced to my parents, "I know what (fill in the blank) means." After nearly swallowing their forks, my parents calmly informed me that we would discuss it after we had eaten. The discussion that followed was awkward, embarrassing, and helped to set the groundwork for years of sexual shame and struggle. I remember being particularly confounded by the actions of my prolific grandmother.

"You mean Nanny had to do it FIFTEEN TIMES?"

Gary and Marie Ezzo write, "(We believe) Sex education is the primary responsibility of the parents. No one can do the job better than properly trained parents, for they are the only ones who have the right to determine what value system is placed into the hearts of their children." [3] If we hand our children over to modern culture, or entrust them to the "sex education" agenda of strangers, we are irrevocably passing the baton into undeserving hands. Once our children receive sexual information – or misinformation – from an outside source, it is difficult, indeed, to undo the damage. On the other hand, if our own sexuality is not grounded in modesty, respect, and self-love, then we will be doing our children the disservice of passing on our own unhealthy perceptions and practices. A parent who desires to pass a healthy, moral sexuality on to his child must possess the same.

Sex is a wonderful, intimate part of our marital relationships. It should be our desire and goal to raise up our children in a sexually healthy climate, free from the sexual pollution of today's culture, so that they can one day experience sex as the beautiful expression of marital love that it is meant to be. In the meantime, let us allow our children to be children. To everything there is a season; let this season of childhood be a season of innocence.

It's a Dog's Life

I hate dogs.

It may have something to do with the fact that my father, a letter carrier for thirty years, was bitten ten times during his career. Visions of my daddy's leg with a small chunk taken out of it didn't do much to endear me to the canine species. On the dogs-versus-cats scale, I am definitely a cat person.

Herein lay the problem. Because of Eric's severe cat allergy, I had to get rid of my felines (instead of my husband) years ago. I was opposed to the yard-pooping, bath-requiring alternative. And Jonathan was fast approaching the age at which I felt it was important for a child to care for a large pet.

What was a dog-hating mother to do?

The phone call that answered my dilemma came on a cold, January day. "I'm getting a French bulldog puppy!" my neighbor Mindy chirped excitedly. "I was wondering if Jonathan would be able to take him out during the day to do his business."

This was not a question to be taken lightly by an avowed dog-hater! Assuring Mindy that Eric and I would discuss the matter, I hung up the phone and began to ponder the implications. Involving Jonathan in the upbringing of a puppy would undoubtedly affect our entire family. What if Jonathan decided, halfway through, that dog-sitting was not his life's calling? Would I find myself standing in the rain watching a dog relieve himself on my neighbor's lawn? Did I really want to put myself in the position of having to bear responsibility, like a sort of surrogate mother, for a hapless, un-housebroken French bulldog?

In the end, it seemed to us that giving Jonathan such an important task would ultimately serve to teach him a level of responsibility that might not otherwise have been reached. And so, several weeks later, the children and I bundled up, crossed the street en masse, and went to visit, for the first time, baby Jake.

For those of you who have never had the privilege of meeting a French bulldog, I feel compelled to inform you that they do not look very much like dogs. Indeed, Mindy had warned me that Jake was more akin to a baby pig than a dog, but it wasn't until I saw that squooshed face and fat belly that I actually believed her. Jake didn't bark, either; he snorted. And in the midst of all that pot-bellied, squoosh-faced snorting, my son fell in love with a puppy.

For the first week, I accompanied Jonathan on his twice-daily jaunts to Jake's house. Mindy, in her wonderfully sequential way, had outlined a precise routine for Jonathan to follow. Jake was to be removed from his crate, taken outside, given a drink, played with, and put back into his crate with one or two doggie-treats (broken into little pieces, of course). As each day passed, I watched Jonathan become more and more comfortable with both the dog and the routine. I found I had to will myself to back off and let Jonathan do even the more challenging tasks, like stepping into the play yard (the sides of which were as tall as Jonathan's legs) while holding Jake. I felt myself smiling (me! the Dog Hater!) as I watched Jonathan and the puppy relating to each other. And I was caught a little off-guard when Jonathan announced, after less than two weeks, that he was ready to do the job alone.

Alone? My eight-year-old didn't need my help?

Indeed, as the weeks went by, Jonathan became more confident and comfortable with his task. It was soon clear that, for him, this was a labor of love. Jake, in true puppy-style, had wiggled and snorted his way into Jonathan's heart, where he took up permanent residence. I rarely had to remind Jonathan that it was "Jake Time." Jake had become the love of Jonathan's life.

I had made it clear to Mindy at the start that this was not to be a "paid job" for Jonathan. It was important, I explained, for Jonathan to learn acts of service. "Of course," I clarified, "if you ever want to give him something because it's on your heart, that's fine." (She must have had that "I want to give him something" look on her face.) Sure enough, her thankfulness for Jonathan's help was expressed time and again by all manner of thoughtful gifts. (Even her husband jumped on the wagon and baked a batch of cookies for the kids one afternoon.) Each gift was left on the kitchen counter, accompanied by a little note.

Jonathan has saved every single note.

Truly, everything went smoothly for weeks on end. I felt that, yes, I could handle dog ownership – as long as someone else owned the dog. Day by day, I watched my little boy blossom into a responsible, loving caregiver. Secretly, I began to entertain thoughts of buying our own French bulldog.

Until the day that Jonathan came home with a severely concerned expression on his face.

"Mommy, I think Jake has diarrhea," he announced in a tremulous voice.

My first order of business, of course, was to make sure that Jake hadn't had diarrhea on my son's hands or clothes. (Yuck -- dog germs!) Once Jonathan had clarified that the messy dog poop was in Jake's crate, I called Mindy at work to let her know about her puppy's ill health. Like a concerned mother, Mindy canceled her afternoon appointments and came home.

The diagnosis? Rabbit droppings.

"Are you serious?" I squealed into the phone. "Your dog eats *rabbit poop*?"

"Oh, it's a delicacy for a lot of dogs. Sam used to eat them all the time. I just can't seem to keep Jake from eating rabbit poop every time I take him outside!"

That did it. There was absolutely no way that I would even consider owning a pet that delighted in feasting on the feces of other animals and then having the runs all over my house. Forget it! Surrogate pet-ownership would have to suffice. Jake was awfully cute – but I was more than content knowing that his intestinal upheavals were occurring in Mindy's house instead of mine.

Still, I remain intensely grateful for the dog-sitting experience. Not only has it benefited my son, but it has deepened our relationship with our neighbors, which to me is an invaluable gift. Jonathan has left his own little gifts for Mindy on the kitchen counter, along with notes in his best cursive handwriting, and Mindy has extended her gift-giving to include my three other children. My phone conversations with Mindy have grown from five-minute dog information exchanges to one-hour, intense-girl-talk sessions. My entire family has learned what it's like to share our lives with a sweet, comical dog, and my little boy's life has been enriched beyond my expectations.

Who would have dreamed that a dog could accomplish all that?

Neighborhood Children

"Wait till I tell you this one," my neighbor grumbled. I smiled inwardly, knowing I was in for another bout of complaining about other children in the neighborhood.

It seems that my friend had left her two sons in the care of a twelve-year-old who lived across the street so that she could take a one-hour walk. Sounds harmless, doesn't it? Yet no sooner had she left than the four-year-old from across the street arrived - unsupervised and wielding a full-sized shovel.

Shortly, three more neighborhood children arrived and embarked on wild play inside my neighbor's garage. The shovel-swinging delinquent caused some damage before the twelve-year-old was finally able, with the help of my neighbor's eight-year-old, to disband the crowd. The four-year-old terrorist's mother only came to collect him because she was ready to run an errand.

My neighbor was annoyed, to say the least.

I tried to muster an ounce or two of sympathy, but it was a struggle. Quite frankly, I felt that she had brought it on herself. How, you ask? First of all, by leaving her children with someone who was too young to demand obedience, and secondly by having an open-garage-door policy in the first place.

"But I want my children to be able to plaaaaay with the other kids," she'd whine. And so she quickly established the reputation of "Mom With Open Garage and Cooler Filled With Juice Boxes." She soon learned that the more she gave, the more was taken - and the empty juice containers were left scattered on her garage floor. Resentful, but driven by guilt, she complained while continuing to enable the same behavior to repeat itself over and over again.

No child in this neighborhood had better appear uninvited inside my garage. If he does...I'll send him packing.

"I can't wait until some children move in up there and play in YOUR garage!" my neighbor petulantly announced.

"There won't *be* any children playing in my garage."

"Oh, yes there will," came the All-Knowing reply.

Excuse me! I expect my children to make phone calls or ring doorbells if they wish to play with a neighbor's child, and I expect the same from other children. I reminded my neighbor that I didn't show up in her garage when I wanted to chat with her. At least I got a momentary chuckle from her.

My children are social beings. It didn't take them long, for instance, to fall in love with the three children who moved next door to us this spring, and beg to play with them whenever they were outside. Long before then, though, my little suburbanites could be found chatting with our empty-nester neighbors or hanging out with the young married couple across the street. They also enjoy shouting Spanish words to the Mexican construction workers on nearby sites, and love to tell me how the men "grinned" at them and said "hola."

In short, my children are not isolationists.

I sometimes think - and I'm sure it must be so - that some of the mothers on our street assume that I am not interested in socializing my children. Since I can't exactly respond with, "Well, actually, I just don't want them to socialize with *your* children," I will have to have another answer at the ready. And I do.

Here is the truth: I am protective of my children. I will not allow them inside the home of someone I do not know well. I will not encourage them to play with children (without my supervision) whose parents I do not know, or whose apparent lifestyle or values clash with my own. Does this make me unfriendly? Antisocial?

Nope.

You see, I make the choices concerning my own children. Those choices aren't made by my neighbors or by other children. And I am not one of those mothers who lets her children roam the neighborhood with nary a check-in call. Call me neurotic if you want to; I prefer to describe myself as wise.

In the past year, I have seen young children roller skating down a steep street amidst construction traffic, clambering on the foundation of a home in between foot-high protrusions of rebar, climbing inside a trash-filled dumpster, and engaging in unsupervised "sword fights" with large sticks. Where are the mothers? Where are the boundaries? And why in the world would I want this pack of unruly youngsters congregating at *my* house?

Don't get me wrong. I love children. I am one of those women who wanted to be a mommy since the age of three. My background includes teaching four-year-olds in a daycare and teaching music in an elementary school. To me, children are one of the greatest joys of living.

There is a vast difference between teaching our children to be friendly and teaching our children to be *indiscriminate* in their choice of companions. While my children certainly attend birthday parties to which they are invited and love to play with the other children at our neighborhood picnics, I am not inclined to set them loose with children who may very well speak more negatively than positively into their tender lives. Do I really want my children hanging out with kids whose mother doesn't seem to care if they play with axes? Is it wise to allow my children to play with others whose parents think it's all right for them to watch PG-13 movies? And do I really want my backyard to be the neighborhood hangout, so that other, less vigilant moms can use me as a free baby-sitting service?

No, thank you. And I won't be serving juice-boxes at my garage door, either.

"Good fences make good neighbors." It is an old adage, yet it stands true. I delight in reaching out to the folks who live near me, and I enjoy getting to know them. It feels good knowing that there are many people whom I could call in an emergency, and many who would not hesitate to call me. In the end, though, it is healthy boundaries that keep our relationships healthy. Remember: Saying "no" to a gang of children doesn't make you the Witch of West End Avenue. It does make you, though, a wise neighbor who knows the importance of setting the rules of fair play.

My back yard in not a playground, my garage is not a gym, and my children are not available to amuse the boredom of other children in the neighborhood. But ring our doorbell - and my children will be happy to share their swing set with you. Give us a call - and perhaps we can schedule an afternoon of play. If we will all teach our children to respect our neighbors' *time and property,* we will all get along better.

And by all means - don't send your four-year-old across the street with a shovel.

Family: Surviving vs. Celebrating

"Traveling" or "How To Avoid the Road Trip From Hell"

My parents live eight hundred miles away.

In some ways, the distance has been good for our relationship. My mother and I, for instance, are a volatile mix of "exactly-alikeness" and "different-planetness," so the space and distance help us to appreciate one another. The downside is that neither one of my parents is a particularly avid traveler. Consequently, it has been left to my husband and me to ensure that we get together regularly. Although my parents do travel at least once a year to see us, we have done our fair share of traveling as well.

Before the children came along, it was easy enough to hop in the car and make the drive north. In our younger, more adventurous days, we could make the trip in one day. Adding Jonathan to the road trip merely constituted the addition of an overnight stay at a hotel, thus breaking the trip into two shorter, more manageable stints. The easiest time to travel with a child is, after all, before he is potty trained. Nothing is quite as easy as pooping-in-transit. Nursing an infant is never a problem, either; when it's time to nurse, any roadside stop will do.

When Maggie was born, we remained undaunted. Traveling with two wee ones wasn't much different than traveling with one.

Until the assault of the chicken pox.

It was a day or two before our scheduled departure from my parents' home. We had noticed two round, red bumps on the side of Maggie's face, but had come to the conclusion that they were mosquito bites. Oh, the folly of wishful thinking!

Several hours into our trip home, we stopped for lunch at a burger place. It was during our meal that I noticed the red spots all over Maggie's scalp.

"Here's another one. And another one!" I was shrieking. "Oh my gosh, they're all over her head!"

Eric shushed me and instructed me to gather everyone up so that we could quietly leave the restaurant. I'm sure the other families preferred to dine without the risk of their little ones contracting chicken pox.

We slept in a hotel that night, until around 3:00 a.m., which is when we had decided to leave for the last stretch. It was easier to get three or four hours of traveling in while the children were sleeping. Little did we know that, on this trip, there would be no sleeping.

Thirteen-month-old Maggie cried incessantly. She was feverish, itchy, and miserable. Whenever her crying would wane for a few minutes, we held our breath, hoping that she would finally doze off. It never happened. To make matters worse, every time Maggie began to cry, three-year-old Jonathan started to scream. Not cry – scream. At the top of his lungs. He was so exhausted and stressed out that he just couldn't take it anymore. Neither could I. I closed my eyes and stuck my fingers in my ears, trying to wish away the entire scene. Eric drove on – doggedly, white-knuckled.

Try to imagine the scenario. It's 5:00 in the morning. For the past two hours there has been a constant cacophony of crying and screaming in the confined space of a Toyota Camry. And there are still five hours of traveling left.

We swore we would never, ever drive to Pennsylvania again.

Foolhardy duo that we are, we did make one more road trip. By this time, Rachel had been born, and had taken Maggie's place as the youngest member of our caravan. To avoid long stretches in the car, we decided to make the trip in three days instead of two. Think of it: three days of traveling each way. That's almost an entire week eaten up with traveling.

That was the end of our driving days.

To those of you who think flying with young children is an impossibility – think again. I have come to view Southwest airlines as my personal shuttle to the North. The short trip and lowered stress is worth more than the cost of airline tickets, which is considerably lower for us because of my husband's skill at finding excellent rates online.

Our first "family flight" occurred when the children were five, three, and almost-two years old. We sat in one of Southwest's "extrovert" seating arrangements; that is, three seats facing three other seats. It was like having our own, private cabin on the plane. The children were thrilled beyond measure to be flying in an airplane, and Eric and I were thrilled that we'd be landing in less than two hours.

I don't claim to lose my "tightly wound" status on these excursions; at least not until we are safely seated on the plane. My husband has the irritating habit of going to the bathroom right before the announcement to board the plane. The last time we flew I was frantically flagging him down as he made his way back from the restroom. He was lucky he held the seating passes, or I may have simply boarded without him.

One of the biggest advantages of traveling with little ones is the privilege of pre-boarding. I try not to look smug as I hustle past the other passengers with my cute, pint-sized cargo in tow, heading for the seats of our choice. I almost think it would be worth continuing to have babies until menopause, just to keep our pre-board status. I once found myself almost resenting an elderly woman in a wheel chair because she got to pre-board before we did. She may have been handicapped, but she didn't have to herd four squiggling, excited tots into the airplane with her!

The actual flight is almost always smooth sailing. The children love to look out the windows and eat their little bags of honey-roasted peanuts and raisins. Even the bathroom offers a source of fascination for little girls who simply cannot hold their pee-pee until we land.

Of course, there was the time that Jonathan threw up five minutes into the flight. Fortunately, I was seated with the girls across the aisle. It's disconcerting how useless a husband can suddenly be rendered. There Eric sat, panicking and hollering, "Jonathan says he feels like he's going to throw up!" I yelled back, "Grab a barf bag!" as I started to frantically search for one myself. Eric, of course, had no idea what a barf bag was, and by the time I offered mine, it was too late. Jonathan's breakfast was all over his sweater, his seat, and the floor.

"Eric! Don't you know what a barf bag is?" I exclaimed as I rang for the airline attendant.

Jonathan was fine for the rest of the trip; the smell of fuel had made him nauseous, and once he'd been cleaned up he was ready for a second breakfast (which, of course, we did not allow him). My firstborn had always been an enthusiastic flyer, and he recovered quickly from this minor setback.

Our most recent flight included Spencer, bringing our traveling party to a total of six. Despite a pile of luggage a mile high, a barely-walking toddler, and enough childish energy to wear out the most stalwart traveler, we came through it unscathed. After so many successes at airports and in flight, we have been loath to ever again attempt the fourteen-hour drive to Grandmom and Grandad's house.

Lately, though, I have been toying with the idea: "Eric, I think we should try driving up again. We could break it up into several days and stop along the way to see interesting things. I really think we could do it. What do you think?"

All he really has to say is "chicken pox." That shuts me right up.

Love Fest

My children have no idea what a cupid is. And yet, in our home, Valentine's Day comes in at a close second to Christmas.

It started innocently enough. Several years ago, it occurred to me that my children would never experience the traditional decorating of Valentine boxes and passing out of Valentines that I always enjoyed doing while in elementary school. (A quick disclaimer: this moment of nostalgic weakness is in no way a negative reflection on our decision to homeschool.) I decided that it would be even more fun to start this tradition at home.

Determined to create The Perfect Family Valentine Box, I cut a thick slit in the top of a large box, and decorated the box with hearts and lace. I then helped my little ones make Valentines for each other and for Daddy. All the Valentines that we received in the mail went into the box as well. I also added little gifts, such as candy and small toys. On Valentine's Day, after a special meal, we sat down on the floor, emptied the box, and opened all our Valentines. The delight on my children's faces was more than I ever could have imagined.

Over the years, our annual Valentine Box has taken on a life of its own. A week or two before the big day, gifts start to arrive in the mail from my parents and sister. I take a small budget and stretch it into as many thoughtful little gifts as I can. As my children have grown older, they have delighted in sneaking Valentine surprises into the box for each other. By the time Valentine's Day arrives, the box is stuffed to capacity.

This isn't about "getting stuff," though. My philosophy of the holiday is simple and forthright: "We are gifts from God to each other, and we are in love with each other. So today, we celebrate that love." There is no mention of romantic love (except, of course, between Mommy and Daddy) or mythological critters bearing spell-inducing bows and arrows. I am merely seizing the day as an opportunity to revel in our love for each other.

Part of our celebration includes a Valentine-themed meal - a tradition started by my own mother, who always served pink mashed potatoes and a heart-shaped meatloaf on the special day. Although my personal bent is toward the extravagant, I have found that the simplest effort produces delight in young children. My little sweethearts have squealed over a heart-shaped brownie (baked in a heart-shaped pan, of course); pink macaroni and cheese (believe it or not, the noodles absorb food coloring added to the water in which they are cooked); heart-shaped cookies, and of course the quintessential heart-shaped meatloaf. And, naturally, no Valentine meal would be complete without strawberry milk or red punch in fancy glasses.

Why am I sharing the details of our family's Valentine's Day traditions? It is simple, really. I want to encourage you to view life with your spouse and children as an ongoing opportunity for celebration. We are all yearly inundated with the commercialization of the "big" holidays. Any holiday can quickly lose meaning if we simply go through the motions because it's expected of us. Grabbing every chance to make a day special will fill your life, and the lives of your family, with more meaning. Husband and wife are priceless gifts to each other. Children are priceless gifts to their parents. To me, reminding each other over and over again, in ways large and small, how much in love we are, is vital to the emotional health of the family.

My husband, who had never viewed Valentine's Day with any particular regard, has expressed to me year after year how special I've made the holiday, and how it has so much more meaning to him now. Isn't that one of our roles as mothers and wives – to create memories for our families? At any rate, it is something I take great delight in. I do not claim to be some sort of Holiday Prima Donna; indeed, you might not find anything remotely exciting in our family celebrations. Yet my family is blessed, and the memories are invaluable. I count that as a great success.

You may be thinking, "But-but-but I expect a dozen roses and a romantic date with my husband on Valentine's Day. Don't we deserve that?" I will be the first to agree that every marriage needs a commitment to special, romantic time together. I am attempting to point out, however, that abandoning the commercialized expectations of our culture brings greater freedom to our lives. Unless you happened to have been married on the fourteenth of February, what significance does that date have in your marriage? Do you really want to fight the crowds at the restaurants? Are you honestly thrilled to receive a box of candy that your husband probably picked up on the way home from work? Are gifts that we "expect" as much of a blessing as those we don't? Wouldn't it be more exciting to receive an impromptu bouquet of flowers in the middle of July, simply because he was thinking of you? There are so many things that we do because "we've always done them" and "everyone does it this way." Just imagine how much more fun it could be to think and live "outside of the box."

Intrigued? You, too, can put aside society's Valentine trappings and claim the day as sacred for your family. Children who are used to receiving open declarations of affection grow up openly expressing it as well. My heart is full as I watch my little ones receiving love notes from one another, and then wrapping their arms around each other with jubilant abandon. This is love, indeed! Take hold of every opportunity to celebrate the relationships within your family. The rewards are immeasurable.

When Mom is a Friend

"Mirror, mirror, on the wall, I am my mother after all."

I recently found this quote stitched onto a pillow in a catalogue, and I laughed out loud. No matter how much I deny it, I do find myself wondering if I am actually a clone of my mother. It's true that I physically resemble my father, but there are moments at which I am indistinguishable from the woman who gave me birth. My husband will attest to the fact that my inflections, gestures, and even reactions are so like my mom's that it's almost frightening.

One of our more quirky traits is the fact that, when my mother and I are laughing and trying to talk at the same time, our voices get higher and higher until the words become completely unintelligible. When my mother does it, my father mocks her, making her laugh all the harder. When I do it, my husband mocks me, making me laugh all the harder. I have given up trying to determine whether or not this is a genetic trait. After all, laughing at ourselves is a healthy pastime.

There was a time in my life when I would not have felt complimented by the fact that I so resembled my mother. She and I have walked our rocky path, and have come to our current state of endearment through honesty and forgiveness. Because we have established healthy boundaries in our relationship, we are able to enjoy each other on a new level. She and I do not always understand each other (despite our quirky similarities, we are in many ways cut from different cloths), but our affection is steadfast. Having stood by me while I've made decisions in my life that were outside of her ken, my mother has become a constant source of support and encouragement for me. I love her dearly, and cannot imagine my life without her.

The birth of a child creates an identity shift in the lives of two women: mother and daughter. As daughter becomes mother and mother becomes grandmother, both women's roles are drastically redefined. When the foundation of the mother/daughter relationship is healthy and stable, the dawn of these new roles can launch a whole new dimension of friendship and camaraderie. While a daughter will always be a "daughter," she must learn to evolve past the role of forever seeking mother's acceptance and approval. Mother, too, must learn to let go of her "mommy grip" in order to allow her daughter to be fully her own woman. When this occurs – voila! Mother and daughter can now be friends.

I credit my own mother with giving me my first revelation about infant care. When my firstborn was one week old, Mom came to spend a week with us. There is no way to accurately describe the sheer joy of watching my mom meet her grandson for the first time – it was love at first sight. On her second day with us, I was just putting Jonathan back down in his crib after his morning nursing, when she gently said, "You know, you could let him have a little awake time before you put him back down."

Fancy that! I didn't have to put my baby back to bed right after his nursing. I don't know why the thought had never occurred to me, but as soon as my mom said it, it made perfect sense. She, to this day, pooh-poohs the importance of her advice, but it was vital information that had, to that point, escaped me. My mother had worried, I think, about her ability to offer me much in my new motherhood, mostly because she had not breastfed beyond a few weeks, but also because she had never had any boys. Little did she know that she was destined to save her grandson from social annihilation!

For me, becoming a mom has helped me to understand the love that my mother has for me. It is no longer hard for me to understand why she spends so much money on my birthday, or why she still delights in stuffing my stocking at Christmas. I may not agree with all of her parenting techniques, and I may even have been hurt by some of them, but I can finally understand where she was coming from. We have both struggled with displaced anger, impatience, and long, boring days of housecleaning. We both know what it's like to be awakened at night by a sick child, challenged to feed a family on a modest budget, and frustrated by the constant clutter that surrounds creative children. We are, in the truest sense, kindred spirits.

Yes, mothers and daughters truly can be friends. Where there is mutual trust, respect, and affection, there will always be friendship. Beyond the role of Doting Grandmother is the equally precious calling of My Daughter's Confidante. I will count it an honor when my own daughters one day consider me their friend.

Besides, "Friend" doesn't sound quite as old as "Grandmother."

When Mom is Not a Friend

For every woman who has a good relationship with her mother, there is another, less fortunate woman who is grappling with her own version of "Mommy Dearest."

A friend once told me the story of a woman whose mother was cold and verbally abusive. Often she would lament to her daughter that she regretted having adopted her. One day, the mother spouted off a string of obscenities in the woman's home, in front of her children. The woman quietly informed her mother that she did not want her children to hear language like that. "They're going to hear it anyway!" was the surly response. "Yes, they will," replied the woman, undaunted. "But they don't need to hear it from their grandmother."

A single woman whom I know personally has such a controlling, manipulative mother that she no longer spends holidays at home. Her mother, although having been confronted with her verbal abuse and manipulation, denies any wrongdoing and insists on her "maternal right" to be loved and respected. It is very difficult, indeed, for this woman's daughter to muster any warm feelings for her. During her annual Christmas Day Phone-call last year, this mother asked her daughter the loaded question, "So, do you miss your family?" How could her daughter possibly answer truthfully without being hurtful? We do not miss that which does not bring us pleasure.

There exists in many families an unspoken rule that "because we are Family, we are okay with each other." In other words, there is an assumption that because someone is our parent or grandparent or sibling that we are automatically in relationship with him. What this assumption fails to take into account is the fact that close relationships are the outcome of mutual respect, affection, and honesty – not of the happenstance of birth. With this "We Are Family" rule in place, many mother/daughter relationships are reduced to nothing more than duty and obligation. Mother "expects" and Daughter "complies," and on it goes.

My own mother is not the kind of woman who demands or expects certain "rights" as a mother or as a grandmother. The "We Are Family" rule does not apply to us, so my mother and I are free to have a healthy relationship. For instance, I do not invite my parents for a visit because I am obligated to, but because I WANT to. While bowing down to the golden idol of Family Obligation, many women fail to realize how much they are compromising. Instead of loving companions, mother and daughter are reduced to respectful acquaintances or, at worst, bitter enemies.

What do we do, then, if Mother is not a loving ally? What if she is harsh – demanding – meddling – or simply cold and distant? How do we fill that "mother space" in our lives – or do we even need to?

The first thing to remember is the importance of setting boundaries. If your mother has the habit of inviting herself over to clean out your refrigerator and refill it with the food *she* thinks you should be feeding your family, do you allow her to continue to do so? If she ignores the rules you set for your children when she baby-sits, do you let her watch them anyway? Or if she belittles you for the choices you've made as a wife/mother/daughter, do you let her words affect your perception of yourself? If you answered "yes" to any of these questions, then you have not set boundaries for what is acceptable behavior.

I recently read an account, in a woman's magazine, of a young mother who frantically brought her four-month-old baby into the pediatrician's office, convinced that the brown threads in her baby's feces were worms. The pediatrician calmly informed her that they were banana fibers.

"That's impossible," claimed the woman. "My mother watches her and she knows not to give her anything except the breastmilk I've pumped." However, when questioned, the offending grandmother confessed: she had felt compelled to feed the baby bananas because she had started her own children on solids at four months.

Why would a woman feel "compelled" to do something that was expressly against the wishes of her daughter - and without having any intention of telling her? What if she had fed the baby something that caused an allergic reaction? Is this the way to have a trusting, honest relationship? Did this woman have the "right" to make a choice like this, simply because she was the baby's grandmother? I am outraged.

Even in warmer, more loving relationships, we need to stand firm: "I know you'd like to give him some ice cream, Mom, but he's only five months old and we're not letting him have any sweets yet." "I'm very proud of the fact that you've been a school teacher for thirty-two years, Mom, but yes, we are going to homeschool our children." And even, "I know my husband exasperates you sometimes, but I need to ask you not to complain about him to me – I love him just the way he is." It is actually possible – and indeed, it is necessary – to affirm and honor our mothers while at the same time setting boundaries.

What if our mothers are emotionally or physically absent? My own maternal grandmother died three weeks before my parents were married. My mother has often shared with me how keenly she felt the absence of her mom, particularly during her own years of raising little ones. How important it is to grieve the loss – to feel the empty "mother space" – and eventually to move beyond it. Likewise, the absence of a mother who is emotionally distant must also be grieved. We must free the little girls inside of us from their constant quest to be loved and affirmed by their "mommies." That time of need has come and gone, and as mature women we must step forward and allow the healing of our past hurts to come to fruition. Accepting the fact that things perhaps aren't the way we'd like them to be will help to ease us along this difficult road.

Yes, mothers and daughters should be friends. It is often not so, however; and, blunt as this may sound, it is not the end of the world. You can be a mom without your own mother's instructions. You can be a wife, a friend, a woman – you can be anything you have been called to be, without your mother's acceptance or approval. Forgive her, honor her, but do not allow her to cast a shadow over your life. I grieve with you for your loss, but I do not despair. If you can get beyond the "We Are Family" rule, you will finally begin to experience freedom.

As for your own daughter: begin now to establish an honest, respectful relationship with her. Humble yourself before her and ask her forgiveness when you have hurt her. Be a good listener whenever she talks to you. Love her unconditionally. You will then have a fighting chance at being your grown daughter's friend – and what a sweet reward that will be!

Imperfect Parenting

Where's Maggie?

It was a delightfully sunny April morning. The baby was down for her nap, and the weather was perfect for my two older children to play outside on the deck. I seized the opportunity and simultaneously reached for the iron and the phone. Killing two birds with one stone and no interruptions -- truly a mother's paradise.

As I removed creases and chatted with a friend, I casually glanced through the windows of the French door to count two blonde heads. One......one....wait a minute, I don't see Maggie. "Hang on, Cathy, I can't find Maggie." I carried the phone with me outside, thinking perhaps she had wandered off the deck into the back yard.

"Jonathan, where is Maggie?" I asked my unconcerned, not-quite-four-year-old son.

"I don't know."

Now my heart began to race. "Cathy, I've got to go. I can't find Maggie."

Down went the phone. Within the next minute I moved from worried to frantic. There were no fences between properties, so I was able to quickly scan to the left and right to see if Maggie had toddled one way or the other. She was nowhere in sight. I ran next door and pounded on the door. Our neighbor's grown son answered.

"I can't find my daughter!" I gasped. I don't know what I expected him to do, but within seconds he was out the door searching. I ran back to my own house and dialed my husband's work number.

"Linda, please get Eric. It's an emergency!" The seconds on hold were minutes of agony.

"Eric, I can't find Maggie anywhere. She was out back playing with Jonathan and I can't find her!"

I can only imagine what Eric was feeling as he listened to my terror-filled words. He assured me that he was leaving immediately to come home. Abandoning the phone, I ran outside, calling frantically for Maggie.

Across the street in my stocking feet I ran, calling and calling. Jonathan, by this time confused and frightened, followed me into the front yard, and when he heard me yelling, he started to cry. I was not capable of comforting him at this point, although I tried to answer him as calmly as I could. I reassured him that we would find Maggie very soon, and that he could help me look.

In the midst of my wild searching, a car pulled over, and a woman my age leaned out and said, "Is something wrong?"

"YES! I can't find my daughter. She's 23 months old and she's wearing an orange sweat jacket."

The woman, who was a mom herself, as evidenced by the tell-tale car seat in the back, offered to drive around the neighborhood and look for Maggie. I was overwhelmed with gratitude.

I felt myself spiraling downward, downward. This couldn't be happening! Jonathan seemed more composed at this point than I. He looked at me and said, "I will look in the house for Maggie."

"Yes, yes, you do that, sweetie."

Then again, maybe I should do the same. Perhaps – just perhaps – I may have overlooked her.

I raced into the house and tripped up the stairs. The bedroom door was closed. I opened it and froze in the doorway.

Maggie was asleep in her bed.

It all came back to me then. She had been unusually tired, so although her regular naptime wasn't until after lunch, I had put her down for a little rest. Then I promptly forgot about her.

I rushed over and scooped her into my arms. Suddenly awake, she looked at me bewilderedly as I squeezed her and kissed her and thanked the Lord that she was safe. How could I have forgotten where she was? Oh, the sweet relief of the moment swept over me like a wave of pure joy.

Until I remembered that two neighbors were out scouring the area for my lost daughter.

Now came the really fun part: humbling myself in front of two good Samaritans who were spending their time looking for nobody. At about this time my husband came rushing in. Having made the usual fifteen minute commute in about eight minutes, he was rather bug-eyed, though much more together than I had been.

"I found her. She was asleep upstairs the whole time." Then I dissolved in tears in his arms.

After pulling myself together, I ran outside to find my kind neighbor.

"I found her! She was asleep upstairs the whole time. I'm sorry!" I flashed him a sheepish grin.

"Oh, that's all right, the same thing happened to my parents when I was little!" Sure it did.

The last thing to be accomplished was to find the nameless lady in the car. Eventually she drove around again and I confessed for the third time that, yes, indeed, my daughter had never been lost in the first place. And of course I had to tell it all one more time when my friend called, worried and wondering what had transpired since I'd abruptly hung up the phone.

"I found her, Cathy. She – was – asleep – upstairs."

Two years later I went to a yard sale, and the woman who lived there looked at me long and hard. Then she said, "Aren't you the lady who thought she lost her little girl?" These things have a way of following us.

But oh, the ecstasy of knowing that your child is safe. I will gladly accept the title of Scatterbrain of the Year while I hold my precious daughter in my arms.

Goof-ups

Children are resilient. They were designed that way, I am sure, as a safeguard against the occasional lapse of intelligent consciousness by one or both parents. Regardless of how protective and vigilant we are, there will come the inevitable moment of parental shortcoming. Wise is the parent who prepares himself ahead of time for the unavoidable slip-ups that come with the territory.

Incidentally, I am not talking about gross negligence. There is never any excuse for purposeful neglect or injury to a child. I am referring, rather, to little incidents that make us question if we are, indeed, sane enough to continue along the precarious journey of parenthood.

I take you, as an example, to a warm, early summer evening in our little two-bedroom ranch home on Agatha Court. Eric was drowsing on the sofa with infant Maggie lying on his belly. Jonathan, two years old, was playing on the floor, and I was engrossed in a pile of brownie recipes that my mother had mailed me. In the midst of my chocolate reverie, I was startled by a knock at the back door.

Since the main room in our home was a "great room" with the front door at one end and the back door at the other, I had only to look up from the sofa to see who was knocking. Imagine my surprise when I saw that it was…Jonathan.

"Eric! Jonathan's at the back door!" I exclaimed, as I ran to unlock the door. How did he get there? How in the world did my toddler end up on the back deck?

After a few moments of complete befuddlement, I noticed the front windows. Both were open to let in the warm, evening breeze. One of them was missing the screen. Upon looking out the window, I saw the screen lying on the bushes. It became immediately clear what had happened: Jonathan had fallen out of the front window.

The immediate question is: How in the world did two grown-ups fail to notice a two-year-old child tumbling out of a window? I have no rational answer. Fortunately, it was no more than a two-foot drop to the garden below, and, assuming that Jonathan had landed on the bushes, the fall had been even shorter. He was completely unscathed by the incident.

The remarkable part is this: Jonathan, at the tender age of two, had had the presence of mind to pick himself up and walk around the house to the back door, where he proceeded to knock so that we would let him in. Such presence of mind is not often seen in adults, and I marveled at my son's pragmatism.

Losing track of children seems to increase in direct proportion to the total number of children. One Sunday several years later, we rushed home to beat the arrival of the people in our church group, whose meeting we were hosting. The first guests had arrived, and I suddenly realized that I didn't know where Rachel was. Since she was less than two, I was immediately concerned for her safety. The children didn't know where she was, and she didn't answer my calls. I frantically asked Eric if he knew where Rachel was.

"Didn't you get her out of the van?" was his response.

"Eric, I thought YOU got her!" I yelled as I ran toward the garage door. As I flew down the steps into the garage, I could already see Rachel's sweet face through the windshield. I rescued her amidst profuse apologies and kisses. The incident had so traumatized her that she had ceased crying by the time

I arrived. I held her close as I tearfully imagined her frantic cries, and how she must have felt when nobody answered her. The fear that she would be emotionally damaged for life threatened to engulf me with remorse.

Of course, when questioned a few years later about whether she remembered the incident, Rachel looked at me blankly and said, "No."

Maggie, on the other hand, has informed me that she clearly remembers the time that we left HER in the van. This time we were all stopping off at Eric's office while he attended to a small amount of business. We hustled everyone out of the van and across the parking lot. When we arrived at Eric's third story office, I said, "Where's Maggie?"

A few, panicked moments later I had rescued a teary-eyed but grateful four-year-old from the locked vehicle. The vision of Maggie sitting helplessly in the locked van as she watched her family walking obliviously away across the parking lot was too much for me. "I'm sorry" didn't begin to express what I was feeling. Yes, Maggie had been unharmed, but what of the emotional impact of having been left behind?

Thus I have come to a stark, painful truth of parenting: We are going to make mistakes. And worse yet – our mistakes will have an emotional impact on our children.

I believe that yelling at children is wrong; yet I sometimes yell. I believe that answering children in a tone of voice that conveys annoyance is wrong; yet I often answer that way. Clearly, even with the best intentions, I am bound to succumb to human frailty. The perfectionist in me wrings her hands in despair; the wise mother in me humbles herself enough to ask forgiveness.

How willing my children are to forgive me! How freeing it is to know that, even when I have done something wrong, they will immediately afterward open their precious hearts to me in complete abandon, as if to say, "Mommy, I don't care if you're not perfect. I love you anyway!"

What good will it do us to play the "Queen Mother" role in our children's lives? Construction on walls of resentment begins early, brick by brick, by parents who will not admit wrongdoing to their children. When we freely forgive our children their wrongs, and humbly ask their forgiveness for ours, we are establishing a solid foundation of respect and trust upon which our relationships will continue to be built.

Of course, my children's forgiveness does not preclude the fact that I have deserved nomination for "Dingbat of the Year" several times already. Somehow, forgiving myself is harder than saying, "I'm sorry." The grace we need to receive from our children needs to be generously bestowed upon us by ourselves as well: "Okay, Jill, you have definitely messed up. Your kids have forgiven you. You're not perfect. Now, I forgive you."

Let us strive to continually better ourselves while at the same time allowing for error. Letting your baby roll off of the changing table (been there, done that) or forgetting to secure the car seat to the back seat (am I blushing?) may not qualify you for "Mother of the Year," but moving on from there as quickly as possible, while having gathered, perhaps, an extra measure of wisdom and experience, is the best thing you can do.

Perfect mothers? No such thing. By God's grace, we will do our very best. If our "best" is seasoned with humility and a vigorous sense of humor, we will be successful, indeed. Our children will survive our occasional lapses of sanity....and so will we!

Mother or Screaming Banshee?

Sometimes I yell at my children.

It is painful for me to admit it. From the depth of my being, I believe that it is wrong to yell at a child. Yelling produces nothing but anger, fear, and resentment. Yelling is among the Top Three Demons of verbal abuse (the other two being manipulation and character-bashing).

Yet sometimes I yell at my children.

I was yelled at as a child. My mother was yelled at when she was a child. I can only assume that my grandmother and her mother before her were yelled at when they were children. Yelling is one of those nasty things that we hand down from generation to generation. We learn by example that yelling produces action; that yelling is an acceptable way of venting anger; that yelling is what mothers do when children disobey. We enter the wondrous arena of motherhood declaring that we will not parent the way our own mothers did - and we end up yelling anyway.

But it doesn't have to be this way.

A friend of mine once described to me how a woman she knew had the habit of going into a closet or back room and screaming into a tea towel when she was stressed. After venting into the unfortunate towel, she would rejoin her children. In this way, she avoided responding inappropriately to her little ones. I marveled at this woman's wisdom and self-restraint. It is so much easier to blow a gasket without thinking about how it is affecting our children's tender spirits.

Despite the wisdom of this woman's tea towel ritual, I believe that there is more to dealing with yelling than simply training ourselves to scream privately. There are deeper issues at work here that cause yelling mothers to continue yelling. Yes, yelling is a bad habit that we learned as children - but underneath the habit, compelling it to continue, is unresolved anger.

Some of us are angry with our mothers. Some of us are angry with our husbands. And some of us are angry about a plethora of other things.

Now, I am not trying to play psychologist. It's merely a fact that a person who is not angry will not yell.

"But my children MAKE me angry, and I yell at them! It's hardly my mother's fault!"

Of course it's not your mother's fault. And it's not my mother's fault, either. If I am yelling at my children, it is my own fault, for not dealing with my issues and learning to respond appropriately to stressful situations.

Here is a classic scene from my life: Eric and I get off on the wrong foot from the moment the alarm goes off. He dawdles in bed and ends up running late. As a result, he once again misses having breakfast with the family, which has become a ritual of high importance to me. I am furious at his lack of responsibility, and barely give him a nod as he rushes out the door. Ten minutes later, the children start arguing at the table. I turn on them and yell, "A-A-A-A-A-ALL RIGHT!! STOP FIGHTING RIGHT THIS MINUTE OR YOU WILL ALL LEAVE THE TABLE AND SKIP BREAKFAST!" There are a few seconds of stunned silence, and then the clinking sound of spoons hitting cereal bowls begins to ring out. Trembling, I leave the kitchen and run upstairs to the bedroom, where the tears start to flow.

I wasn't really angry with the children, you see. I was angry with my husband for failing to meet my expectations. When the children started arguing, they didn't need for me to yell at them. They needed me to intervene firmly and lovingly to set their behavior on the right track. Instead of helping them learn to get along, I vomited my anger all over them, and left them to cope with the aftermath.

It wasn't their fault. It wasn't even Eric's fault. It was my own.

What do I do when I have lost my grip? I ask my children to forgive me. And the part that never ceases to amaze me is that they always do - willingly. The grace they allow me far surpasses the grace I allow myself. They know that I believe that yelling is wrong, for I have told them so. I do not want them to grow up believing that it is all right to yell simply because Mommy does it sometimes.

As I continue to walk this path of dealing with latent anger, I can look back and see how I have grown. I can honestly say that I am less likely to yell now than I was three or four years ago. Still, I will not be satisfied until I see myself consistently avoiding responding in displaced anger. My children are far too precious to be subjected to my uncontrolled fury.

"A gentle answer turns away wrath, but a harsh word stirs up anger." (Proverbs 15:1)

We all need some "time out" once in a while. After all, this full-time mothering thing takes a lot out of us! If we are ragged, tired, burned out - we are so much more likely to yell at our little ones. If screaming into a tea towel works for you, then do it!

For another, it might be a brisk walk or a phone call to a friend. A whirlpool bath usually works wonders for me. But it's important to remember that in addition to providing stress outlets for ourselves, we also have to be willing to look at the root sources of our anger. It may not be pretty - but it will be worth it.

I don't have to keep yelling at my children. You don't have to keep yelling at your children, either. Nobody's perfect - but there is clearly no reason to continue a habit that is detrimental to our children's emotional health. Together we can find the courage to face the anger source, the wisdom to diffuse stress, and the humility to ask our children to forgive us when we hurt them.

A mom who is willing to learn, change, and grow is a wise mom, indeed!

Eating Crow

I have come to realize that "eating crow" is part and parcel of being a mother. How have I come to this conclusion? It's simple, really. You see, women who have not started their families yet tend to have rather big mouths when it comes to issuing opinions on other people's offspring. Since women who *do* have children used to be women who did *not*, it follows that most mothers, at some point in their pre-mothering or pre-toddlering or pre-adolescenting days, decreed a statement or two beginning with "I can't believe she..." or "I would NEVER...", only to later find herself in exactly the same situation she once so vehemently denounced.

I should know. It seems to be a recurring nightmare in my own life.

When Jonathan was still my one-and-only, endlessly brilliant and incomparably adorable child, I encountered a woman in the supermarket one day whose baby girl was waving "bye bye" the wrong way. How absolutely stupid, I thought. The dumb child is waving at herself. Why doesn't her mother teach her the right way to wave? No child of mine would ever display such a lack of common intelligence.

A year later, I beheld my own daughter Maggie waving contentedly at herself.

Then, of course, there was the absolute contempt of children-with-dirty-faces that I had held since my high school days. Time and again I could be found secretly sneering at children whose cheeks displayed their last two meals, rolling my eyes at babies sporting twelve-inch drool strands, and backing away in disgust from crusty little noses that were thick with snot. Never! I swore. Never will I allow my children in public places looking like *that.*

As I gaze lovingly at my own children's smeared little faces, I can only shame-facedly repeat that yes, indeed, eating crow is definitely a main ingredient of motherhood.

While a dirty face may or may not reflect a woman's mothering skills (she may not have yet discovered the mess), an issue of discipline almost always does. And I have always been most harsh in my assessment of the behavior of other women's children.

"Do you see the way she's letting her children run down the aisles? I would NEVER let my children do that!"

"Listen to those two boys fighting. Why hasn't she taught her children to get along?"

"Look at that toddler standing up in the shopping cart. Can you BELIEVE she's letting her do that?"

On it goes. I am quite sure that, had I put my mind to it, I could easily have written a 500-page book entitled, "All The Bad Things Other Children Do That I Will Never Allow Mine To Do." Of course, were I to write the book *now*, I would be compelled to call it "All The Bad Things Other Children Do That I SWORE Mine Would Never Do."

Take, for example, the time I attended a meeting of our local homeschooling field trip group. The situation was less than ideal - one big, ugly room in the back of a library, the four walls of which were lined with various animal heads mounted on plaques. There was no separate room for the children, so the noise level was ridiculous. At one point I shushed several rambunctious boys nearby, who, rather than obey, glared at me

205

as if to say, "And just who do you think *you* are?" Where were their mothers, anyway?

I was nearly at the end of my rope when suddenly one of the women called out, "Whose little girl is that? She shouldn't be touching those!" I glanced in the direction of her wagging finger, and there, to my horror, was my own Maggie, standing on a chair, reaching boldly for the nearest moose-head.

"Maggie! Get down!"

My daughter's immediate obedience was severely eclipsed by the fact that she had touched the moose-head in the first place. In the midst of all that chaos (I don't know how the other mothers could stand it), *my* daughter was singled out for being intrigued by a dead animal head. I could hear the voices in my mind: "Can't she control her children?" "I can't believe she didn't see her daughter climbing up there."

The voices, of course, were nothing more than my own conscience barking back at me. The other mothers in that deafening crowd probably didn't give me a second thought.

Crow meat really doesn't taste very good. In fact, it's quite rancid.

If only I could remember to give others a measure of grace before passing judgment so ruthlessly. Sometimes we have bad days; sometimes our children have bad days. If one mother's overly tired toddler is throwing a fit in the grocery store, it may very well be my turn the next time. Quietly observing the ineffectiveness of buying a chocolate bar for a screaming child would be better than rolling my eyes and shaking my head in contempt. It is true that, having been a mother for many years, I am more prone to sympathy than I used to be - especially for women with more than two children in tow. Still, from time to time I will observe what appears to be the worst behavior exhibited by any child on the planet, and I find myself once again falling into the "I can't believe her children are acting that way" mode. Then I can rest assured that the crow will be back on my plate before long.

To all the mothers I've scoffed at over the years: I'm sorry! It's really none of my business how you raise your children. If you are having a difficult outing with your children while I am enjoying a pleasant one, it is quite possible that the tables will be turned the next time. And if your children are always unruly, I do not need to comment on that in light of my own imperfections. It is good, I think, to encourage, correct, and admonish each other - but not to point fingers in accusation.

Now, if you will excuse me, I need to go polish my children's halos.

Precious Moments

Dancing With Rachel

The classical music crackling from the minute speaker of my alarm clock radio beckons my 4-year-old daughter from the third floor. She glides into the room as if transported on a length of silk.

"Did you hear the music from all the way up there?" I ask. She nods dreamily.

I attempt to make the bed while she rolls on it, and finally shoo her off onto the floor to play with the baby. She silently obeys, bestowing wet kisses and watchful eyes on him, ever mindful that she is older, bigger; his protector.

The music changes. It is a passionate piano piece.

"Mommy, dance with me."

I struggle for a moment with the thought of abandoning my tasks. It is difficult – so very difficult – to find uninterrupted time in which to accomplish the mundane but necessary. The moment of struggle is just that: a moment. It is soon over, and I walk away from the mundane to indulge in the necessary.

I dance.

Our hands meet, and I close mine over her sweet, sweaty ones while we spin. The music crescendos; we part and twirl, reconnect, and part once again. I imagine that I am a fluid, graceful song in motion. My daughter has lost herself in the abandon of the dance. I lose myself along with her.

I am sweating; my heart is beating in my throat; still I dance. I feel my face melting into a broad smile, even as I pant for air.

We are liquid joy, my girl and I. There is nothing that can come between the dance and us.

We are the dance.

It doesn't matter that I am stiff, awkward, out of breath. In my daughter's eyes, I am a ballerina. And she is a fairy princess: sweet beauty on tiny feet. Dance, little one.

The music ends; I curtsy. My daughter, recognizing my posture as some sort of finale, runs over to me.

"Let's dance some more, Mommy."

To her, there is no time constraint, no schedule, no end to the dance. I smile and tousle her hair and tell her that I am too tired to dance another dance. She whines a little whine, the corner of her rosy lips scrunched up in a disappointed tuck.

Life fleets; life hurries; life dances. My daughter has brought focus to my day, and a dance to my soul.

Keep dancing, sweet daughter. Dance in your heart; dance in your spirit. May your life be one long, continuous dance. Whenever I can – whenever you need me to - I will dance with you.

Thank you, my little one, for this dance.

Angel of the Sea

My honeymoon was a flop.

Well, maybe that's a little harsh. It's true that I was deliriously happy to be married to Eric, and no matter where we had gone, I would have been traveling in a cloud of marital bliss. Our honeymoon, though, was a kind of last-minute, throw-it-together thing, instead of the carefully planned excursion I would have preferred. We opted for a simple honeymoon because we had decided to use our wedding money as a down payment on our first home. As a result, we didn't have much to spend on our little, unplanned get-away. So we left the afternoon after our wedding for the shores of Cape May, New Jersey, with two suitcases and no hotel reservations.

"Oh, we'll find a place to stay once we get there," Eric assured me. Silly me - I trusted him!

We found a place, all right. My second night as a new bride was spent in a filthy motel that sported cigarette burns on the side of the bathtub. I didn't even want to crawl under the sheets! When morning dawned, I begged my new husband to take me somewhere else - somewhere that at least smelled better. Fortunately for him (and perhaps for our marriage), we spotted a "vacancy" sign outside a tidy motel two blocks from the ocean. A short while later, we unloaded our things into Room Seven at the Madison Motel and headed for the beach.

Sounds romantic, doesn't it? Yet I can honestly say that I have never longed for my honeymoon days. I remember having to buy a beach towel because we hadn't brought any, and then sharing it because we didn't want to pay for two - spending an evening on the boardwalk in Atlantic City and getting a painful blister on my foot - and sitting on the bed crying because Eric was watching television instead of showering me with attention. Definitely not the heady, passionate, whirlwind vacation that bridal dreams are made of.

Cape May itself, though, is a quaint town filled with Victorian homes and delightful shops, and Eric and I often said that we'd like to go back some day. Our "some day" didn't come until after the births of four children and the passage of thirteen years - and it was definitely a "some day" worth waiting for.

Having secured our little ones at my parents' house in Pennsylvania, Eric and I settled into our rented van for the three-hour drive to Cape May. Admittedly, I was feeling less than passionate; leaving Spencer for the first time and worrying about my mother's stress level had left me wondering if I was going to be able to relax and enjoy myself for the next two days. By the time we arrived in our favorite beach town, though, I had passed the hurdle of anxiety, never to return to it. The weather was beyond perfect - blue sky, low humidity, and gentle, ocean breezes. As we pulled up in front of The Angel of the Sea - a beautiful, Victorian bed and breakfast that I had for years been longing to visit - I knew in a heartbeat that this vacation was going to immeasurably surpass our honeymoon.

Truly, I do not have words to adequately express the joyful intimacy that Eric and I shared during the two days that followed. "The Angel," a magnificently restored building with wonderful porches and gables, was a Victorian paradise. Our room was on the third floor, with an ocean view. The floors creaked; the staircase leaned to the right; the pedestal sink had separate faucets for hot and cold water. High tea was served at 4:00; wine and cheese at 5:30. Eric and I reveled in the romantic ambiance of the place, and in the pleasure of not having to share each other with anyone else during our stay. We dallied on the porch, strolled on the beach, and dined at two of the finest restaurants we've yet encountered. As each escapade drew to a close, we would look at each other and say, "What do you want to do next?" Oh, the freedom of not having to take a five-year-old to the bathroom, change a diaper, or dispel a sibling argument!

Beyond the obvious, "three-days-without-kids" feeling lay an inexpressible delight in each other. Had it really been that long since we gazed into each other's eyes? Was it possible that we could have so much romantic fun after thirteen years of marriage? The intensity of our enjoyment of each other was unlike anything we had experienced before. We both felt as though we had reached a new level of intimacy, and agreed that we would carry it with us when we left.

I blush to confess that I used to argue with Eric that it wasn't necessary to "go out" in order to foster a closer relationship. "If our relationship isn't that great at home," I'd insist, "then what makes you think that a night out is going to make it any better?" I couldn't have been more wrong. While it's true that we do need to enjoy each other's company all the time, there is definitely something to be said for getting out of our every-day habitat and rediscovering each other. Our Cape May adventure did more for our marriage than anything we've ever done. More than just a "night out," it was an intensely precious, two-night extravaganza that revitalized our marriage and united our spirits on a level we had not yet experienced.

Do I dare say more? Should I risk sounding incredibly corny by expounding on the delight of spending a romantic holiday with the love of my life? I am so much more than just the mother of his children! I am his wife - his lover - a woman whom he finds incredibly sexy, and whom he spoils at every opportunity. Knowing that I am precious to him makes it remarkably easier to face another day of peanut butter sandwiches, math lessons, and pee-pee accidents. Finding myself in his arms at night softens the roughest day. The importance of our connection to each other must not be minimized: we are truly one.

If love, like fine wine, truly does improve with age, then I cannot fathom its depths twenty or thirty years from now. From the emotional immaturity of our honeymoon days, Eric and I have struggled, like a woman giving birth, through years of trial and pleasure, pain and blessing, to emerge stronger, wiser, and more deeply in love. We have not "arrived;" we are not finished growing. But we are more committed than ever to our marriage, and to the priceless gift of two inextricably entwined hearts.

Thank you, Cape May! You have not seen the last of us.

Good-bye, Crib

During my fourth child's second year of life, my baby accessories began to fall apart one by one. First, the tray to the high chair would no longer clasp on, so it had to be discarded. Next, the pad of the collapsible playpen grew lumpy, rendering the entire thing useless. Outfits that had survived four babies suddenly wore out. The crib mattress sagged in the middle.

Eric perceived the entire process as prophetic: "We are finished having babies."

For me, it wasn't so clear. Sometimes I would agree; after all, our quiver was full and our baby items had paid for themselves four times over. On my more introspective days, I would hold tenuously to the fact that I was still young enough to have another baby, and wouldn't it be fun to have all new baby things?

Then it happened. Spencer, whose development timetable had been consistently later than his siblings', climbed out of his crib. He was twenty-one months old.

At the time, it was quite funny. Spencer had been in his nap for an hour, and the girls had just gone outside for some fresh air. I heard applause and laughter emanating from the front yard, and moments later Jonathan marched in to inform me that the girls were playing with Spencer.

"Spencer's in his nap," I replied in my "know-it-all-mommy" voice.

"Yeah, but the girls are playing with him — he's awake," Jonathan persisted.

More curious than annoyed, I glided out the front door. Immediately, Maggie excitedly informed me that, not only was Spencer awake, but he was standing by his window, looking out.

"He's out of his crib!" she exclaimed.

Spencer's bedroom was on the second floor, facing the front of our house. It was not unusual for him to be distracted by outside noises during his nap, and, in his babyish curiosity, to reach across his crib rails and pull back the curtain to peek out. I assumed that this was what he was up to, and informed my older children quite confidently that Spencer was still in his crib. After admonishing them to stop commanding his attention, I made my way upstairs to investigate.

Spencer was standing on the floor, by the window.

I was simultaneously enthralled by his cute determination and chagrined that he was not only still awake, but had been roaming around his room for the past hour. After tucking him safely back into his crib and reminding him that it was nap time, I went about my usual business, looking forward to sharing this latest development with Daddy that evening.

That night, after animatedly telling the story of Spencer's First Escape, I was caught completely unprepared for Eric's immediate and matter-of-fact response: "Well, I'll go take the crib down."

"Take the crib down? Why do you have to take the crib down?" There was a frantic edge to my voice. It was obvious from the look on Eric's face that he did not comprehend my angst.

"Jill, we have to take the crib down. We've always taken the crib down after they've learned to crawl out. It's a safety thing."

I knew that. Of course I knew that! At the moment, though, I was not thinking of safety or "what we always did." I was thinking that, in a few minutes, there would no longer be a crib in Spencer's room. The thought horrified me.

"But Eric," I tried to explain. "When we've taken the crib down before, I've always assumed we'd put it up again some day. This time....this time..." I could hardly bring myself to say it. "This time could be the last."

If I thought that this sentiment would in any way soften Eric's determination, I was wrong. Within fifteen minutes, the crib was dismantled and stored away. Spencer's little mattress was on the floor in the corner of his room.

My life had suddenly become crib-less.

Spencer's sisters were squealing with delight over their baby brother's new "bed." Maggie wanted to give him her pillow. Spencer himself was crowing with self-importance as he marched across the mattress and flung himself down upon it, grinning ear to ear. I, however, sat dazedly on the floor. Spencer's room felt emptier. It was missing the one thing that had kept him still my "baby."

The crib was gone.

I am not a woman to arrogantly declare that I am finished having children. In this age of convenient birth control and "family planning," it is not unusual for couples to decide how many children they want, and stick with their numbers. I, however, am reluctant to admit that my childbearing years may well have drawn to a close. Life has its rhythms, and mine has been pulsating for some time in strong, four-beat measures.

I am in the midst of a great ambivalence. I catch a glimpse of my breast pump paraphernalia on the top pantry shelf, and I shudder and groan. On another day, I see footage of a newborn baby on television, and I weep with indescribable longing. Is this a rite of passage for all women, or is it me? Knowing how chaotically full my life is, how can I even begin to entertain thoughts of having another child? Daily, I waver between the taste of a new measure of freedom and the desire to lay my life once again on the altar of utter sacrifice. Deep in my spirit I know that there is a part of me that will forever long to give birth and nurture infants. On the cusp of a new season of life, I find myself desperately clinging to the dream of another baby, and desperately wanting to move on.

To my husband I say, "Handle me gently, my love. My mommy-heart is aching for another child while my woman-self is yearning to move onward. Let me cry; let me dream. Then, tenderly, help me to let go."

Good-bye, crib; you have served me well.

Endnotes

[1] Shel Silverstein, "Thumbs" from <u>Where the Sidewalk Ends</u> (Harper and Row, 1974), p. 68

[2] Gary and Anne Marie Ezzo, <u>Reflections of Moral Innocence</u> (Growing Families International Press, 1992, 1995), p. 7

[3] IBID, p. 12